RELATIVE DIVIDEND YIELD

Relative Dividend Yield

Common Stock Investing
for Income and Appreciation

Anthony E. Spare
with
Nancy Tengler

JOHN WILEY & SONS, INC.

New York • Chichester • Brisbane • Toronto • Singapore

Recognizing the importance of preserving what has been written, it is a policy of John Wiley & Sons, Inc. to have books of enduring value published in the United States printed on acid-free paper, and we exert our best efforts to that end.

This publication is designed to provide accurate and authoritative information in regard to the subject matter covered. It is sold with the understanding that the publisher is not engaged in rendering legal, accounting, or other professional services. If legal advice or other expert assistance is required, the services of a competent professional person should be sought. *From a Declaration of Principles jointly adopted by a Committee of the American Bar Association and a Committee of Publishers.*

Library of Congress Cataloging-in-Publication Data

Spare, Anthony E.
   Relative dividend yield: common stock investing for income and appreciation / Anthony E. Spare.
      p. cm.
   Includes index.

   ISBN 0-471-53652-0

Printed in the United States of America.

10 9 8 7 6 5 4 3 2 1

Printed and bound by Malloy Lithographing, Inc.

To my wife, Eleanor, and my children, Alex, Samantha, and James

Without their help and support I would not have written more than a few pages.

Preface

TWO PROFESSORS AT TUFTS UNIVERSITY were particularly influential in my undergraduate years and led, indirectly, to the development of the Relative Dividend Yield approach to common stock investing. One was the chairman of the Economics Department, Dr. Lewis F. Manly, who happened, by a lucky chance of the scheduling in my freshman year, to be teaching the introductory course. I knew nothing of economics then. Since my father, Alexander T. Spare, was an attorney and a businessman, I had had some exposure to the real world where economics is reflected in actual practice. But, beyond a few preconceived notions, I had no sense of how the system is supposed to function in theory and practice. Professor Manly, in his sixties then and dead some years now, was a superb teacher of the basics. Although a Harvard-trained classical Keynesian, he had the ability to look at those basics in a very objective and straightforward manner. His course fascinated me, and thus I decided to major in economics.

The other strong influence in my undergraduate days was Dr. Harry B. Ernst. His arrangement with Professor Manly was such that he had to teach only three courses instead of the normal load of five. Every afternoon he ran a stock market advisory service. Dr. Ernst, who is still active in investment research in the

Boston area, taught the business statistics course. He questioned the conventional wisdom. His course was very real-world oriented, not theoretical, and he was quite cynical about statistics.

The higher the level of economics courses I took, the less meaningful they became. They had little to do with the real world. I realized, as I went through the course work, that somebody was trying to put into quantitative terms what just cannot be reduced to numbers. Distortions of reality were creeping in, and Dr. Ernst's groundwork—his instilling in me a healthy suspicion of numbers and assumptions—allowed me to recognize them.

One example will always stick in my mind. I clearly remember how Dr. Ernst stated the problem, where I sat in the classroom, and where the person who came up with the right answer sat. It involved ten years of monthly retail trade statistics. We were given all the data. Ten years of monthly results involved a lot of computations (we had no computers), and we were asked to come back to the next class with a seasonally adjusted monthly factor for retail trade. There is a considerable amount of seasonality in retail sales with sharp increases and decreases happening repeatedly. The formulas for the calculations were in our textbook, but, again, this was in precalculator days. It was quite a project, and a special challenge to the liberal arts majors, who did not know how to use a slide rule because they considered it a tool strictly for engineers.

The right answer to the problem was that it could not be solved with the data given. Easter, a very important holiday for retail stores, falls in either March or April. Without knowing the timing of Easter, the project could not be done correctly. That opened my eyes to the need to challenge numbers—or, at least, to be very aware that you have to try to understand what is behind the numbers.

I went on to a project of my own that dealt with help wanted ads as a leading indicator of economic activity. Presumably, strong demand for new hirings forecasts economic expansion ahead. But I had learned my lesson, and my report dealt with a host of factors— a strike in the auto industry, to name one—that might distort the conclusions reached just from counting the help wanted ads in the newspaper. I knew that you can have all the math right, but the math is seldom enough: You have to question whether or not other factors must be considered. This skepticism has stood me in good stead in looking at numbers alone in trying to make investment conclusions. Such independence is one of the most valuable lessons I learned at Tufts.

At the Stanford Graduate School of Business (GSB), the key person in my professional development was Philip A. Fisher. He was not on the permanent faculty but rather was a visiting instructor during one of the years that I was at the GSB. Mr. Fisher is one of the legendary investors of our time. He is the author of *Common Stocks and Uncommon Profits,* still a bible for growth-stock investors, as well as several other very insightful investment books written in the 1960s. Since I did not think I could "out-Fisher Fisher," I borrowed those elements of investment thought that I believed appropriate and applied them to another group of stocks. Although a growth-stock advocate, he is, nevertheless, also one of the great value investors. He looks not at book value, yields, or revenues related to total market capitalization but rather at what he considers to be the true value of a successful firm. Although the Relative Dividend Yield (RDY) approach to investing is very different from the growth-stock approach of Mr. Fisher, I learned from him how to take a different look at companies and how to think unconventionally about investing.

Moreover, Mr. Fisher taught me a great deal about stock valuation and put in place a framework within which I could build my own valuation thinking. He taught me that companies have life cycles—from the venture stage to the moribund—and, while he likes companies when they are young and growing, I came to realize that opportunities also exist when the companies are more mature. He is an enormously stimulating thinker and teacher. He taught me how to look at the market, why each investor should understand his or her tools, and how to think through the whole investment process. He spelled out the criteria for judging the quality of a company that guide me to this day. He led me to think, too, in terms of time horizons—that is, to have a different time horizon from that of other investors and to take advantage of the ineptness of most of the others in the investment business. Mr. Fisher owns some stocks for 20 or 30 years. He believes that I am a short-term speculator, with five-year holding periods.

In addition, there is an advantage for non-growth-oriented investors in understanding the other, more conventional growth approaches. You have to know and try to understand the other players in the investment game. Probably 90% of Wall Street analysts are growth-stock oriented. Value, cheapness, just is not very important in their analysis. Much of the reason for their attitude is their time horizon. No Wall Street analyst could make a living if a client asked, "What do you think of the XYZ Company?" and the analyst answered, "It's cheap." The client would then ask, "Well, when do you think it will start turning up?" It would be the end of the analyst if he or she replied, "I don't know— in three to five years maybe." All anybody seems to care about now is the next quarter, which is exactly what makes opportunities for the value buyers, whether of cheap growth stocks or cheap maturing companies. It is why it is necessary to understand the growth investor's mentality. If the vast majority of investors are not going to touch a stock whose earnings are predicted to be flat or are up only slightly for the next quarter or two, those stocks are going to be so neglected that their prices will be driven down to a point where the value buyers know they have found an opportunity.

Most investors would be better served by having stocks at both ends of the risk scale rather than doing what most people do— owning the safe stocks in the middle. The idea of the efficient frontier is good to remember: If you do take more risk, the rewards will be greater. So will the volatility, but this is something that investors with long time horizons can bear. There are also, for the individual investor, tax considerations: If you hold the stock of a steadily growing company for 25 years, you do not have to hand over part of your profits every year to the government; your money can compound. Then, too, growing companies pay out less in dividends, which are, of course, taxable income to the individual investor.

There is a place for growth-stock investing and venture capital within the overall investment spectrum. Everyone is a value investor in a sense; growth-stock investors think they are, too. The critical difference is that most of the growth-stock investors' expectations are built into the price of their stocks. Fisher's precepts are still the guide to follow if you are dealing with growth stocks. The equity income approach that I take, which deals with maturing companies and concentrates on yields, is, frankly, not as exciting as growth-stock investing, particularly if you specialize in emerging growth stocks. But the risk is far less, and the rewards are far more certain.

To sum up, from Professor Manly I acquired all the basics, a thorough grounding, an inside-and-out foundation. He brought everything to its fundamentals, simplified as much as possible—and "simple" and "easy" are not the same thing at all. From Dr. Ernst, I learned not to trust consensus thought and always to look behind the numbers. And, from Mr. Fisher, I learned that if you really understand the companies you invest in, then you have the edge over the typical institutional investor, whose time horizon may come from job-related pressures and not from investment considerations. In many ways, the Relative Dividend Yield approach is the result of taking these elements and putting them together in a different fashion. My three mentors contributed to the ideas that led to the process, even though the result is not what they themselves would construct.

After Stanford GSB, I went straight to the Bank of California, where I worked for 25 years before setting up my own firm with colleagues from the bank. I started as a trainee, but I was a failed branch trainee. It seems I was, in my own words, "too mean, nasty, and opinionated" to deal with branch clients. Since these were not bad attributes for the investment management business, I moved to that division of the bank. Eugene H. Gray, head of the trust investment department at the bank, hired me as a junior analyst.

Gray, who has been retired for some time, had joined the bank in 1951 and convinced the powers that be that common stocks would prove a good investment for trust department clients. That was heresy at a bank back then; ever since the Depression, only bonds were considered prudent for a bank's investment clients. Gray was a radical in his time and another individual whose intellectual independence shaped my way of looking at things.

At first, the only stocks the bank invested in were growth stocks, the big, well-known names that soon were to be called the "Nifty Fifty." We did not have many income stocks until the mid-1970s. By that time, I was in charge, serving as head of research and as chief investment officer. Before that, I learned the lesson that led me to the Relative Dividend Yield approach.

When the Nifty Fifty stock prices peaked in the early 1970s, one of the stocks, Polaroid, was devastated. The stock, a premier growth stock at the time with a multiple of 65 times estimated earnings, plummeted from about $150 to under $15 per share. Even if all of my forecasts about earnings had proved accurate (and they were not), the outcome was already reflected in the price of the stock at its peak.

Polaroid forced me to think about value. No matter how good the story, is the potential already reflected in the stock? This question led me to think about the obverse: Regardless of how bad the story, is the outcome already given in the price of the stock?

That is when Ted Shen, an analyst at Donaldson, Lukfin, & Jenrette, put out chart books that concentrated on relatives—relative price to book value, relative returns on equity, relative returns on assets, relative P/Es, relative earnings growth—every aspect of every stock was looked at from the point of view of its relation to the market as a whole. Shen used the S&P 400 for his relative chart book. Back in the early 1970s, there was no computation of book value for the S&P 500, and Shen wanted to include relative price to book value in his research. So, he used the S&P 400. One small piece of these books dealt with relative yield, and it caught my attention.

I have often asked myself why our discipline has worked when so many managers cannot match market returns or even add value. I think a vital reason is that we do have a discipline. *Any* discipline works better than *no* discipline. Managers with a consistent approach to markets are bound to produce better results than managers who stick a finger in the air and try to go with the flow of the moment. Staying with a tool, even if it is an inferior tool, is better than not understanding when to use which tool or not having any tools at all.

I think all the successful investors I have known or read about could explain what they do and how they apply their method. Many investment managers, however, cannot describe how they make decisions. They cannot explain why their portfolios act the way they do during particular economic and market environments. They do not even seem to have a clear focus or defined goals. How can you know whether you are doing something right if you do not know what it is you are trying to do? Defined goals and approaches are necessary whether you are a value investor, a growth investor, a short seller, or even a commodity trader. While I admit that there is "more than one way to skin a cat," I also believe that Relative Dividend Yield is a superior tool and a better way of improving excess rates of return while reducing variability of return.

However, I am sorry to say that, in my observation, disciplines that are thoroughly thought out and adhered to are rare. Many people in the investment business have no clear idea of what they are doing with other people's money. When I started in the investment business 25 years ago, I suspected that 60% of investors did not know what they were doing, that 15% did, and that 25% were at least smart enough to pay attention to the 15%. Today, I am far more cynical and estimate that 85% of investors—particularly professional investment managers—do not use a clear and consistent approach, that 5% do, and that 10% know enough to follow the 5%.

I do not think that individual investors are at a disadvantage in the market relative to most institutional investment advisors. The individual investor, whether he or she has a little money or a great deal of money, is sophisticated enough to develop and stick with a discipline and will have little trouble beating the average institutional investor.

Many investment advisors are perhaps not suited for the business. Many came into the business because investment management is respectable and socially acceptable. The title "investment advisor" has an aura about it. But many investment professionals have no real passion for investing and have never learned much about it. They are thus more "dangerous" than the individual investor because they have more money under their control.

To be successful, an investor must be willing to go against the crowd—that is, to maintain an attitude of skepticism and independence, to have a real-world orientation and to pursue clearly defined goals, and to use consistent approaches within a framework relative to the market as a whole.

Acknowledgments

I WANT TO PARTICULARLY RECOGNIZE the special contributions of just a few of the many individuals who made this book possible. All of my associates at Spare, Tengler, Kaplan, & Bischel must be thanked first. Over the years, their questions and their challenges to my answers have forced me to a deeper understanding of the ideas reflected in this book.

Nancy Tengler, the president of our firm, must be thanked next. Her understanding of what "Relative Dividend Yield" represents as a tool and method for investment decision making is reflected in every chapter. The hours she spent in refining the concepts and presentation of what we have implemented for a decade and a half are reflected on every page.

I am grateful to my other partners, Ken Kaplan and Andy Bischel, for their support during this difficult process of putting on paper the ideas and experiences we have shared over the years.

Some former employees, like Roger Newell, helped isolate the opportunities for using the "Historical Relative Yield" approach while at the Bank of California. Roger and I had worked together for over 20 years. In addition to his principal job of supervising personal trust portfolio managers, Roger cooperated with me on this investment approach. He was able to find some time each day to implement the specific stock ideas needed to make this approach work in the Bank of California's Income Equity Fund. His confidence in these research-based ideas generated by my research staff and myself will always be appreciated. It takes confidence and conviction to implement the unpopular strategic thinking and specific stock ideas of others, particularly in the face of contrary, consensus opinion from Wall Street.

I also want to thank Eugene H. Gray, my first research director, for having confidence in my ability and for encouraging my efforts throughout my career. Philip A. Fisher taught me that an honest and disciplined approach is needed to succeed in the investment business. Although the investment approach described in this book is very different from the one that he has so successfully followed for over 60 years, it contains many of the essential ingredients of discipline and patience.

Kenneth L. Fisher gave me the confidence to even write a book. He helped develop some of the structure of this book by asking me to participate at an early stage in the development of his own two investment books.

Everett Mattlin, a financial writer and editor who assisted me in the preparation of the manuscript, provided the framework and perspective that were needed to catalyze the start and ensure the completion of this book. His incredible ability to sift through hours of taped discussions of RDY at the start of the process is hereby commended.

My editor at John Wiley & Sons, Wendy Grau, must also be thanked for asking the questions that you, the reader, would have asked during the drafting stage.

John Brush at Columbine Capital provided the data used in Appendix B. His objective statistical support of the idea of dividend yield and yield change made an important contribution to the empirical validation of our approach. I also want to thank Joseph O'Connell of Lynwood Associates for his statistical work on the DJIA study in Appendix A.

Finally, I want to express my appreciation to the tremendous support staff at STK&B. Marian Luoma, in particular, spent many hours deciphering this text and the changes made to the various drafts.

Contents

xvii

Contents

RELATIVE DIVIDEND YIELD

Section I

INTRODUCTION TO RDY INVESTMENTS

Introduction

SCIENCE, ART, BOTH, OR NEITHER?

SOME SAY THAT INVESTING is an art and that it has little or nothing to do with numbers. But anyone who is a true artist—a painter, composer, musician, novelist, dramatist, or dancer—would laugh at the notion that investing is an art form. While many investors try to rely on intuition and "feeling" about the market and stocks, very few highly successful investors invest based on emotions alone. When it is well done, investing certainly has elements of craftsmanship to it. You know your tools and how to use them. Both a broad ax and a scalpel are useful cutting instruments, but you would not want to cut down a tree with a scalpel or take out someone's appendix with an ax. Of course, growth-stock investors need different tools than value investors do. But craftsmanship, regardless of how well done, is not the same as art.

Others say that investing is a science. Certainly, true scientists—physicists, chemists, mathematicians—would be just as appalled to hear investing labeled as a science as artists would be to hear investing called an art form. Investment decisions should not be based on rigid formulas alone because the numbers by themselves distort reality and mislead us. Those who think or act as though investing is some sort of rocket science are fooling themselves and their clients. Modern portfolio theory has given the investment world a very useful descriptive vocabulary, but it has not provided very reliable forecasting tools. The quants who do nothing but data manipulations have all of the facts and statistical correlations. What they are missing is an understanding of the meaning of the data in the real world. Correlations and causalities should not be confused. Seeing and understanding are not the same. The computer jockeys who claim they make no forecasts usually are clearly implying that their calculations, based on the past, offer a good projection of the future.

All investment professionals who have been in the investment business for any length of time have learned to describe the past. The challenge for fundamental analysts, technicians, or quantitative analysts is to answer the key question, what about the future? Companies and industries change, and the relationships between companies and industries and the general market's movements also change. You cannot drive a car by staring in the rearview mirror, and you cannot invest by relying on past correlations. Investing is not reporting.

At best, investing is a "soft" social science. It is based on the social sciences—psychology, sociology, and economics—which are not "hard" sciences like mathematics, physics, and chemistry.

If investing rests on the interrelationship of psychology, sociology, and economics, then it can hardly ever be rightfully thought of as anything approaching true science. While many quantitative investors may try to sound mechanistic, mathematical, and scientific, they may also deliver highly subjective reasons why their system does not always work.

It is better to start from the other direction. That is, the investor must first understand that the business of investing is "soft" and then try to add the discipline and patience necessary to succeed.

1

RELATIVE DIVIDEND YIELD: AN INTRODUCTION

DEFINING RELATIVE DIVIDEND YIELD

Let's begin with two assumptions:

1. Investors want to buy "cheap" stocks and sell them when they are expensive.
2. Few investors have ever figured out how to do so consistently over the long term.

Relative Dividend Yield (RDY) is an approach that can be applied, at various levels of detail and sophistication, by institutional and individual investors alike. Although relatively unknown, it is a powerful and intuitively sensible approach to value investing.

A very large number of companies—even among today's most popular stocks—have provided dividend yields that have been higher than that of the market (the Standard & Poor's 500) sometime during the past 30 years. Many have had above-average yields during the past decade. These periods of above-market yield levels have generally reflected investor disenchantment with the future prospects for these companies. Relative Dividend Yield is a good indicator of the level of investor enthusiasm or despair over the investment outlook for many types of issues. RDY allows the investor to identify stocks for purchase whose yield has risen relative to the market and the stocks' own histories, as well as to determine when these stocks become overvalued by watching for the points at which the relative yield falls and the price increases. The key word is *relative,* as you will see.

DEFINING RELATED TERMS

A few simple definitions are as follows:

$$\text{Yield} = \frac{\text{Indicated Annual Dividend Rate}}{\text{Current Stock Price}}$$

$$\frac{\text{Market Index}}{\text{Dividend Yield}} = \frac{\text{Indicated Index Annual Dividend Rate}}{\text{Current Index Value}}$$

$$\frac{\text{Relative Dividend}}{\text{Yield (RDY)}} = \frac{\text{Stock Yield}}{\text{Market Index Yield}}$$

A few examples follow:

	Current Price	Indicated Dividend	Dividend Yield
Stock A	$ 40	$ 1.60	4.0%
Stock B	$ 20	$ 0.40	2.0%
Stock C	$ 60	$ 3.60	6.0%
Index	$300	$12.00	4.0%

			RDY
Stock A	4.0%/4.0%	=	100%
Stock B	2.0%/4.0%	=	50%
Stock C	6.0%/4.0%	=	150%

FINDING RELEVANT INFORMATION

The dividend per share for each stock is the most recent indicated rate, which is the most recent quarterly rate declared by the Board of Directors. The rate is then annualized or multiplied by 4. This is the same dividend level used in the *Wall Street Journal* and *Barron's* as well as the stock tables in various newspapers. *Investor's Daily* does not include dividend per share information on either individual stocks or the market averages because of the publisher's bias against dividend yield as a criterion for stock market investing.

Information on the market's dividend rate and yield is not as easy to find, but it is reported in *Barron's* on a weekly basis and is available through various publications of Standard & Poor's such as *The Outlook.*

9

Figure 1-1 shows a table that appears in *Barron's* every week indicating the dividends and dividend yield for all of the major market indexes. The S&P 500's yield ("A") is based on the most recent price, and current dividend rate ("B") is indicated. Figure 1-2 is an example of the stock tables from *Barron's* that includes the indicated rate ("A"), the current yield ("B") based on the indicated rate and recent quarterly dividend ("C"), as well as the record ("D") and payable ("E") dates. Figure 1-3 shows the *Wall Street Journal*'s presentation of information of indicated rate ("A") and the yield ("B"). Figure 1-4 has dividend ("A") information from a typical newspaper, in this case the *San Francisco Chronicle*.

Some stocks usually have above-market yields. It is only during periods of excessive enthusiasm that their yields are below that of the market. Other stocks have bright enough growth prospects most of the time so that the periods when they have dividend yields higher than that of the market are the unusual periods.

DESCRIBING RDY CHARTS

Before we look at an example, a brief description of the graphs used in this book is in order. There are some common elements to all of the RDY charts. The scale on the side of each graph indicates the Relative Dividend Yield for the *particular* issue. When the RDY is at 100%, it is equal to the S&P 500's yield, and when the RDY reaches 200%, the yield is twice that of the market. The scale for each stock is different, as we will discuss. Time is indicated along the bottom of each graph. The graph line is the RDY using quarterly plot points. The time periods observed are very long. RDY does not require that the investor watch the stock and the market on an hour-by-hour, day-to-day, or even week-to-week basis.

Figure 1-5 shows the RDY graph of a real company, here called the XYZ Corporation. This is a stock whose yield is usually above that of the market. There have been many periods when the yield on this stock has risen far above the market's yield and has entered a range that is high in relation to the stock's own history; therefore, the stock is potentially attractive. By looking at a graph such as this one, a graph that often spans about 30 years, the investor can

FIGURE 1-1

Barron's Indexes' P/Es and Yields

	Last Week	Prev. Week	Year Ago Week
DJ Ind.-P/E	24.8	22.7	11.6
Earns Yield, %	4.02	4.40	8.65
Earns, $	120.07	130.39	207.49
Divs Yield, %	3.10	3.12	4.23
Divs, $	92.50	92.50	101.53
Mkt to Book, %	224.08	222.42	187.90
Book Value, $	1331.52	1331.52	1276.19
DJ Tran.-P/E	Nil	Nil	17.7
Earns Yield, %	Nil	Nil	5.64
Earns, $	(d8.64)	(d19.89)	46.80
Divs Yield, %	1.52	1.56	2.44
Divs, $	18.53	18.53	20.24
Mkt to Book, %	154.83	151.07	109.73
Book Value, $	786.10	786.10	756.10
DJ Util.-P/E	15.1	15.2	13.3
Earns Yield, %	6.60	6.57	7.52
Earns, $	13.98	13.98	15.48
Divs Yield, %	6.57	6.55	7.01
Divs, $	13.92	13.92	14.43
Mkt to Book, %	137.14	137.66	133.09
Book Value, $	154.46	154.46	154.68
S&P 500-P/E	19.60	19.59	14.11
Earns Yield, %	5.10	5.10	7.09
A → Earns, $	19.46	19.46	21.26
Divs Yield, %	3.20	3.21	4.09
B → Divs, $	12.21	12.24	12.27
Mkt to Book, %	243.86	243.73	203.74
Book Value, $	156.42	156.42	147.26
S&P Ind.-P/E	20.77	20.77	14.21
Earns Yield, %	4.81	4.81	7.04
Earns, $	21.69	21.69	24.73
Divs Yield, %	2.78	2.79	3.57
Divs, $	12.53	12.57	12.55
Mkt to Book, %	296.14	296.15	241.86
Book Value, $	152.15	152.15	145.34

DJ latest 52-week earnings and dividends weekly file adjusted by the Dow Divisors in effect at Friday's close. S&P June 30 12-month earnings and indicated dividends based on Friday close. DJ and S&P book values latest available for FY December 1990 and 1989.

11

FIGURE 1-2

Barron's New York Stock Exchange Composite

					A		B									C	D	E
														EARNINGS		DIVIDENDS		
Mkt Sym	52-Weeks High	Low	Company Name	Tick Sym	Div Amt	Vol 100's	Div Yld	Earn P/E	Week's High	Low	Last	Net Chg.		Interim or Fiscal Year	Year ago	Latest divs.	Record date	Payment date
	19⅞	9⅛	Continuum	CNU		193	...	16	13½	12¾	13⅜	− ⅛		Jun3m.10	.17	....	....	....
	13¾	6¾	ControlData	CDA		1623	...	...	9½	9⅛	9¼	− ¼		Jun6mX.34	X.42	Y	....	10-1-85
	42½	32⅞	ControlData pf	CDAp	4.50	z1700	11.1	...	42	40½	40½	−1¼		....	....	q1.12½	9-2	9-30
	6⅞	3¾	ConvtHldg	CNV		3062	...	...	6⅞	6¾	6⅞	+ ⅛		....	....	....	....	....
x	12⅛	9⅞	ConvtHldg pf	CNVp	1.40e	x698	11.8	...	12⅛	11½	11⅞	+ ½	✚	....	....	.38	10-15-91	10-25-91
	19¾	8⅜	ConvexCptr	CNX		5759	...	13	11	10¼	11	+ ⅝		Jun6m.11	.42	....	....	....
	6⅛	2½	CooperCo	COO		1436	...	...	4	3⅝	3¾	− ¼		July9mD.78	D.31	Y	....	1-15-88
	58	31¼	CooperInd	CBE	1.16	10118	2.3	17	51	49⅝	51	+1		Jun6m1.33	1.22	q.29	9-13	10-1
	35	21¼	CooperInd pf	CBEp	1.60	6016	5.2	...	31¼	30¼	31	+ ½		....	....	q.40	9-13	10-1
	36⅞	12⅜	CooperT&R	CTB	.28	6560	.8	21	35½	33⅝	34⅝	− ⅛		Jun6m.77	.73	q.07	9-6	9-30
	8¼	4	CoreInd	CRI	.48	360	8.5	51	5⅞	5½	5⅝	− ⅛	✚	May9m.25	.54	q.12	12-9	1-2
	71½	36⅛	Corning	GLW	1.00	5052	1.5	21	69¼	67⅛	68⅛	− ⅞		Jun24w1.30	1.19	q.25	9-9	9-30
▲	12⅞	9¼	CounselTndm	CTF	.24	204	1.9	...	12⅞	12⅜	12⅞	+ ⅝		....	....	.12	2-22-91	2-28-91
▲	33¾	5⅜	CntrywdCrd	CCR	.40	19742	1.2	25	33¾	28½	32⅞	+2⅝		Aug6m.81	.51	.10	9-27-91	10-16-91
▲	90	20	CntrywdCrd pf	CCRp		863	...	...	90	80	90	+6½		....	....	.5938	9-3-91	9-30-91
	7	4	CntrywdMtg	CWM	.84	1075	12.0	9	7	6¾	7	...		Mar3m.21	.17	.21	7-31	8-15
s	24⅛	11¼	Craig	CRG		195	...	13	15⅞	15⅝	15¾	− ⅛		Jun9m.91	1.32	....	....	...
	17⅜	8¼	Craig prA	CRGp		229	...	7	11¼	9¾	10½	−1		....	....	....	....	...

FIGURE 1-3

***Wall Street Journal* Exchange Composite Transactions, June 13, 1991, p. C3**

52 Weeks Hi	Lo	Stock	Sym	A Div	B Yld %	PE	Vol 100s	Hi	Lo	Close	Net Chg
32⅛	26⅜	BklynUnGas pf		2.47	8.0	...	10	31½	30¾	30¾	− ⅜
12⅝	7⅞	BrownShrp	BNS		...	...	14	8⅛	8	8⅛	...
84½	60½	BrownFormn B	BF.B	2.24	3.1	15	352	73½	73	73¼	...
5⅝	4½	BrownFormn pf		.40	7.4	...	4	5⅜	5¼	5⅜	+ ⅛
28⅜	19¾	BrownGp	BG	1.60	6.0	17	228	26½	25½	26½	+ ¾
30⅞	17½	BrownFer	BFI	.68	3.7	14	8429	18¾	18⅛	18½	+ ⅛
16⅜	6½	Brunswick	BC	.44	3.6	56	2924	12⅜	12	12¼	...
20	11½	BrushWell	BW	.72	5.2	19	130	14	13¾	13⅞	+ ⅛
28	22⅞	BuckeyePtr	BPL	2.60	9.4	10	129	28	27½	27¾	...
16⅜	12¾	BunkerHill	BHL	1.64a	10.4	...	21	15¾	15½	15¾	+ ¼
13¾	10⅛	BurgerKgInv	BKP	1.56	12.7	14	72	12½	12¼	12¼	− ¼
18½	8½	BurlgtnCoat	BCF		...	12	69	17⅜	17⅛	17⅜	...
37¼	22¼	BurlgtnNthn	BNI	1.20	3.2	...	2990	37¼	36⅜	37⅛	+ ⅝
45¼	32⅞	BurlgtnRes	BR	.70	1.6	29	2163	42⅝	42⅛	42½	+ ⅛
16	10½	BurnhmPacif	BPP	1.36	9.1	51	8	15	14⅞	14⅞	− ⅛
2⅞	7/16	BusinssId	BLI		...	...	156	⅞	13/16	⅞	...
		-C-C-C-									
30⅞	14¾	C&S Sovran	CVN	1.56	5.2	33	10873	30	29	29¾	+1
s 37⅛	20½	CBI Ind	CBH	.48	1.6	21	548	29⅝	29⅛	29⅝	+ ⅝
188⅜	150¼	CBS	CBS	1.00	.7	...	918	154¾	152⅜	152¾	−3
1½	**¼**	**CCX**	**CCX**		**...**	**...**	**5**	**½**	**½**	**½**	**+ 1/32**
11¼	1	CCX pf			...	...	z10	1¼	1¼	1¼	...
9¾	5⅝	CDI	CDI		...	16	111	6⅝	6½	6½	− ⅛
2¾	13/16	CF IncoPtnr	CFI	.16	18.3	...	115	15/16	⅞	⅞	...
56¾	33⅝	CIGNA	CI	3.04	6.6	10	851	46¼	45⅝	46	− ¼
7	3⅝	CIGNA High	HIS	.90	13.1	...	278	7	6⅞	6⅞	− ⅛

identify potential opportunities for acquiring a stock during periods of undervaluation when the price is depressed and the RDY is high and for selling it during periods of optimism when the RDY is low. All of this can be determined by looking closely at the stock's RDY history—a very powerful valuation tool.

When the RDY on this particular stock rises to the levels indicated as "buy" levels, investors are afraid. There may be real or perceived problems at the company that have prompted investors

FIGURE 1-4

***San Francisco Chronicle* Dividend Information, June 13, 1991**

52 Week High	52 Week Low	Stock	A ↓ Div	PE	Sales Hds	Last	Net Chg
7 5/8	5 1/2	BlueChp	.77e		483	7 1/2	+ 1/8
53	42	Boeing	1.00	12	6250	49 1/8	+ 1/2
29 1/4	19 3/4	BoiseC	1.52		3836	23 1/4	− 1 5/8
9 3/8	4	BoltBer	.06	11	207	5 1/2	− 1/4
14	7 7/8	BordC pr	1.89e	10	2135	14	+ 1/4
13 7/8	7 1/2	BordCh	1.89e	10	307	13 3/4	+ 1/8
38 3/4	27	Borden	1.14	13	7042	32 1/2	+ 1 1/8
19 5/8	14 1/2	BCelts	2.25e	10	33	17 1/8	+ 1/8
22 1/4	17 3/4	BostEd	1.58	14	1436	21 5/8	+ 1/8
16 3/4	14 1/8	BosE pr	1.46		2	16 5/8	
30 3/8	16 1/2	Bowatr	1.20	11	1210	23	
18 3/8	6 3/8	Brazil			1273	13 5/8	+ 3/8
39 1/4	21 5/8	BrigSt	1.60	15	326	38	− 1/2
48 1/2	17	Brinker		34	281	46 7/8	− 1/4
87 7/8	57 1/8	BrMySq	2.40	23	11909	83 1/2	+ 1 1/8
33 3/4	24 1/2	BritAir	2.07e		1429	34 1/8	+ 5/8
51 3/8	39	BritGas	2.91e	9	714	43 1/4	− 1 3/4
10 3/4	3 1/2	BritP wt			2180	4 1/4	+ 1/4
81 3/4	63 7/8	BritPt	4.89e	12	1997	72 1/4	+ 5/8
27 3/4	19 1/4	BritStl	2.00e	5	1537	20 3/8	− 3/8
74	49 5/8	BritTel	3.23e	11	397	67 5/8	− 2 1/8
16 1/4	3 1/4	Broadln	.20	12	6273	14 1/2	+ 1/2
13 7/8	13	Broadl pf			5262	14 1/2	+ 5/8
44 7/8	29	BHP	1.24e	16	4	45	+ 5/8
12 3/8	6 1/8	Brooke	.56b		x106	7	+ 1/4
4 7/8	1/2	Brooke rt			109	4 7/8	

to drive down the price, increasing the stock's yield. At this point, the stockholders are receiving more of their return up front via the dividend yield to compensate for their fear. Typically, no one on Wall Street will recommend the stock. It has passed through the stages of "love and hate" and is now in a period of neglect.

CONSIDERING WHY RDY WORKS

Why does the RDY approach work? (It only works, it should be noted, on large, maturing companies, as we will discuss in the next chapter.) First, the stock market is a tug of war between fear and greed. Most investors' attitudes about their stocks move from love

FIGURE 1-5

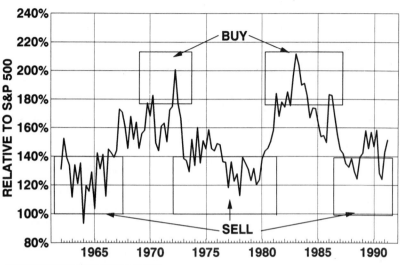

XYZ Corporation, Relative Dividend Yield 1962–1991

QUARTERLY OBSERVATIONS ARE IN JAN, APR, JUL & OCT

to hate to neglect. The problem, clearly, is that the stocks are loved when they are overpriced and should be sold. The way for an investor to make money is to be able to take advantage of these sometimes violent swings in others' emotions. This can only be done with a discipline. RDY is a discipline that allows the investor to step back from the intensity of the emotionalism of the market at important turning points for these stocks.

Second, dividend policy at most large corporations is taken very seriously by management and the Board of Directors. Changes in the dividend are not made without considerable review of the longer-term fundamentals of the company and the industry within which it must operate. Just as the oil companies did not *raise* dividends as much as earnings increased in the late 1970s when oil prices were escalating and profit margins reached unsustainably high levels, so they did not *cut* the dividends in the mid-1980s when product prices dropped sharply and earnings plunged. Our use of dividends provided better information than price-to-earnings ratios (P/Es) based on reported earnings would have provided, and in a much more direct manner. The use of dividends does not require the arbitrary choice of time periods to be averaged to arrive at "normal" earnings, nor does it require assumptions about future profit margins and sales levels.

In addition to dividend yields' providing a discipline that aims at removing the emotionalism of the marketplace, the income stream itself is an important source of an addition to total return. While yields are volatile, moving up and down relative to price, the income stream has been a reliable source of return that grows over time.

Stocks are at their cheapest when they have been neglected by the investment community for a long period of time. When no one is interested in a stock, however, is also often the best time to buy it. Usually, there is plenty of time. Trying to identify the *instant* to buy is not crucial to investment success using this approach. Certainly, there may be some fundamental concerns about the company at this point—after all, you do not get high yield for free—but, as we will discuss, there are some shortcut ways to ensure that you are not buying into a bankruptcy or disastrous situation. One of the best things about buying out-of-favor stocks is that you are always buying from eager sellers.

Now, refer to Figure 1-6, which compares RDY and relative stock price for the same company as in Figure 1-5. Look at the power of RDY as it relates to price. It consistently identifies when stocks are cheap and when they are dear—when the RDY is high, the relative stock price is low, and vice versa. Investor sentiment inevitably changes, however: Today's favorites can easily turn into tomorrow's disappointments, and the company that was neglected by Wall Street analysts for years becomes one of their favorites. The trigger for changing the opinion of the investment community does not matter. What matters is that the patient investor, buying in a period of neglect, now sees appreciation in the stock price as the RDY begins to fall. In the meantime, while waiting for other investors to come around, the investor has been getting paid to wait (via the high dividend income) for sentiment to change.

One of the advantages of this approach is that dividend yield is the method for identifying value as well as the source of an impor-

16

FIGURE 1-6

XYZ Corporation, Relative Dividend Yield and Relative Stock Price, 1962–1991

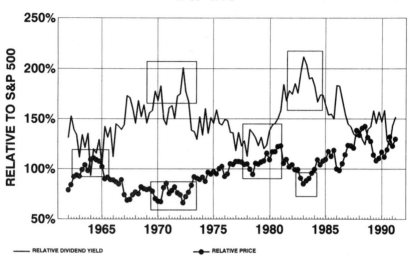

RELATIVE DIVIDEND YIELD   RELATIVE PRICE

Price Index 12/86=100

QUARTERLY OBSERVATIONS ARE IN JAN, APR, JUL & OCT

tant portion of total return. As we will discuss in Section II on building portfolios, the income stream on a portfolio of RDY stocks also provides a cushion in long periods of declining markets.

The approach is not new, or theoretical, or untested. My colleagues and I have been practicing and refining the process for nearly 20 years. Results show that substantial assets managed under the RDY discipline have realized returns that have exceeded those of the market—and with significantly less risk. If an investor can match the market in capital change and generate dividend income 200 to 300 basis points above the market, the returns are compelling.

2

OTHER INVESTMENT METHODS

ABSOLUTE YIELD VERSUS RELATIVE YIELD

Quite simply, absolute yield alone does not work. It does not accomplish the same objective of enhancing investor values as does relative yield. There is not enough information in absolute yield— an investment approach that buys stocks having a dividend yield above some predetermined level. The only way to know whether a stock is truly cheap is to assess its yield against the market's yield and its own past history.

In the early 1980s, almost all stocks had high absolute yields because the market's yield was high. Indeed, the stock market as a whole was cheap. A stock's dividend yield that was far below the market's yield still looked absolutely high by historic standards. In 1982, everything would have appeared cheap to absolute-yield investors because everything had a high yield. The market's yield was above 6%. Then, 5% would have been a below-market yield. Today, 5% is well above the market's yield. Investors must consider yield *relative* to both a stock's history and the market's yield. This is what the RDY approach does.

Figure 2-1 compares absolute yield with RDY for the so-called ZYX Corporation. Several times during the early 1980s, this stock's absolute yield was 5% ("A"). Absolute-yield buyers would have been interested. But, look at RDY ("B"). It does not indicate that the stock was cheap based on history. A 5% yield in a market with a 6% yield is simply not a compelling value based on this stock's history. This case occurs over and over again. There is simply not enough information in absolute yield.

Finally, the arbitrary absolute-yield threshold locked into the absolute-yield process prevents the investor from owning *any* stocks during some very strong markets. When the absolute yields on stocks and the market drop below this yield threshold, there is no indication of "cheaper" or "cheapest." Relative Dividend Yield allows the investor to identify the best values in weak markets as well as in *strong* ones.

Absolute yield has worked with a narrow universe of stocks like the Dow-Jones 30 industrials—but only with such a narrow universe. When absolute yield is applied to a broader universe, however, some industries will almost always dominate the holdings.

20

FIGURE 2-1

ZYX Corporation, Relative Dividend Yield and Absolute Yield, 1962–1991

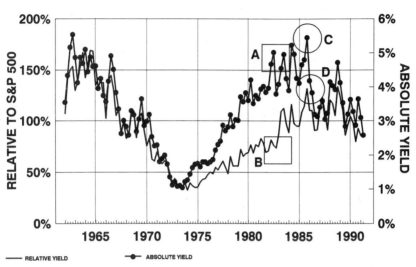

RELATIVE YIELD   ABSOLUTE YIELD

QUARTERLY OBSERVATIONS ARE IN JAN, APR, JUL & OCT

The electric utilities, to cite the most obvious example, usually show up as high-yield stocks. Absolute yield as the sole criterion of attractiveness will not provide a diversified portfolio; it will lead the investor into limited industries and will produce little more than dividend income. Worse yet, absolute yield gives no indication of when these stocks—which always have high yields—might be undervalued or overvalued.

Since absolute-yield investors buy a stock only when it is returning about 5%, 6%, or 7% in dividend yield, portfolios tend to be concentrated in slow-growth industries that always have high yields or, at least, that have had high yields for the last 30 years. Electric utilities, again, are the classic example. They are mature companies; they are regulated; and although their earnings variability is not very high, neither is their earnings growth. The only way to attract investors to stocks like these is by offering a higher current yield. This is the trade-off.

Absolute-yield investors learn quickly that they need to deal with the problem of diversification. Otherwise, they might own

21

only a handful of companies in one or two industries subject to the same fundamental factors. This constraint would result in a high level of variability of return for the entire portfolio despite the high absolute yield of the portfolio.

Like many other methods, absolute-yield investing is faulty as a value indicator, and a whole series of constructions must therefore be installed to overcome the faults. More important than the lack of portfolio diversification, however, is that absolute yield alone does not help investors move in a direction opposite to that of the crowd. Such independence is necessary to make money in the stock market.

OTHER VALUE APPROACHES

Before we examine the RDY discipline more closely, three other approaches to value investing should be discussed:

1. The first is the use of low P/E (price/earnings) ratios. The P/E ratio is, in fact, the most widely employed of all valuation methods in value investing, or among value investors.

2. The second is used by the asset players, those who look at a stock from the viewpoint of the assets available either to be liquidated or on which current management—or new management—could earn more. They look at the price-to-book-value ratio, but they also attempt to forecast what the liquidation value of the assets would be.

3. The third approach is the use of DDMs (dividend discount models). Practitioners of this approach attempt to focus on the future dividend stream, but they can only do so by projecting earnings.

Low Price/Earnings (P/Es) as a Valuation Tool

In trying to establish values, the first question the investor must deal with, philosophically, is, what are we going to look at? The

22

most common answer is, earnings. A low price-to-earnings ratio is probably the most common method employed by value managers.

The followers of a low P/E strategy, however, face a fundamental problem: Either they must exclude very large groups of stocks with cyclical earnings patterns from consideration, or they must override their own criterion of using reported earnings by normalizing earnings.

The cyclicals—the autos, chemicals, papers, oils—are usually at their cheapest in absolute price, and in price relative to the market, when their P/Es are very *high* or even negative when losses are reported. Table 2-1 indicates the problem.

A company that earned $3.00 last year and is reporting $0.50 for this year is not likely to have seen its stock decline by more than 80%. The P/E has gone way up instead. Multiples are high not because investors love the stock, but because earnings are depressed. In fact, they may be negative to infinite. Conversely, when P/Es are low, the prices and reported earnings are often at their peak. If you look only at P/Es as a valuation tool for cyclicals, you will get unusable and misleading information.

What is more, a much larger number of stocks have cyclical characteristics than is generally acknowledged. As one clear example, far more of the Nifty Fifty stocks of the early 1970s turned out to be cyclical in earnings than the adherents of a stable earnings-growth approach thought possible at the time. Cyclicality is widespread and becomes more likely as a company grows, matures, and is more influenced by the overall economy.

Low P/E investors, then, either ignore all cyclicals and look only

TABLE 2-1

Low P/E Cyclical Trap			
Point in Cycle	**Earnings**	**Price**	**P/E**
Earnings doing well	$3.00	$45	15.0×s
Earnings doing poorly	$0.50	$20	40.0×s
Earnings about normal	$2.00	$45	22.5×s
	$2.00	$20	10.0×s

at companies with stable earnings or ignore *reported* earnings or they try to *normalize* past or future earnings. If a company's earnings are down, what is its norm, its trend earnings? Some low P/E investors accomplish this determination by taking an average of the previous five years of earnings. Others look at earnings for certain time periods that include, for example, a recession and a period of expansion. Still others use far more complex formulas that consider revenue growth, gross margins, R&D as a percentage of revenues, normalized pretax profit margins, returns on equity and aftertax returns on equity, leverage employed to realize returns on equity, and so on.

The point is that if low P/E investors do not simply ignore a large number of stocks, then they have to try to normalize earnings so that they can apply their valuation technique. Either you avoid dealing with an important source of value stocks, or you make major adjustments in your process.

Presumably, the low P/E approach should work on stable growth stocks, but since most of these stocks usually sell at premium multiples, the low P/E investor cannot touch them. This eliminates another group of stocks and reduces portfolio diversification. The low P/E investor faces a whole series of problems because P/E by itself will not work when the investor uses reported earnings or does not apply special rules to get around the problems.

As discussed, there are all kinds of ways of arriving at a number that represents normal earnings power. But as will be pointed out in the next section, dividends represent a proportion of normal earnings power. The best way to determine normalized earnings is to use a dividend-based, not an earnings-based, investment decision strategy. Dividend payments are a better indicator of what management views the company's normal, sustainable, earnings power to be than are current reported earnings or, more importantly, the estimates of most securities analysts.

Assets as a Valuation Tool

In attempting to buy assets cheaply, investors either do not look closely enough at these assets or use techniques that are fairly crude and unreliable. It takes a great deal of skill and information to find the "true" values. A typical screen for a value player in this camp would include a low price-to-book value—perhaps 0.4, or a price that is only 40% of the book value.

The problem is that the book value is often inaccurate. The value of plants and equipment, for example, may be overstated, most likely because the return on these assets is very low. This has been true in the steel industry. Many plants that were technologically obsolete were on the books at a very high value. Many of the stocks selling at a low price-to-book value deserve to sell there because the value of the assets is overstated. Book value, after all, is nothing more than assets minus liabilities; if you overstate the assets, you overstate the book value. Conversely, other companies have important assets such as trademarks and brand names on their balance sheets at very low values and, therefore, *understate* their true book value.

Like low P/E investors, asset investors have to adjust for the shortcomings of their valuation technique. They say, for example, "Well, you look at price-to-book, but you buy only if other things are there too" (like a P/E below the market's). At least, this would imply positive earnings.

Dividend Discount Models (DDMs) as a Valuation Tool

Despite the fact that the word *dividend* is prominently featured in the name of this approach, dividends and yield have little to do with this valuation technique. Most DDMs are earnings-growth, computer-driven models. A dividend discount model can be applied to a very low-yield or even a zero-yield stock. Dividend discount model advocates will argue that they try to determine what the dividend will be 20 years from now. How can they? They have to fall back on earnings growth. Somehow, it just sounds better—more conservative and responsible—to talk about a "dividend model" rather than an "earnings model."

Dividend discount model practitioners start with earnings, predict the growth of these earnings, and then decide what the payout ratio is going to be at some point in the future. They take the current (often low) dividend rate and forecast what the dividend stream will become based on earnings growth. The stream of projected dividends is then discounted back to the present to come up with fair present value. It does not matter if the estimates of earnings growth come from an analyst on Wall Street, an in-house analyst at an investment management firm, or a consensus figure: There is no consistent history of analysts' ability to predict earnings growth.

While DDMs are often used by the most quantitatively oriented individuals in the investment community, those who shun subjectivity at every turn, these same individuals are really applying very subjective forecasts when they predict the future growth of a company. What could be more subject to error than trying to calculate the future dividend payments of Digital Equipment or Federal Express, companies that today do not pay a dividend?

Although in theory DDMs should be able to work as well as RDY, the input of analysts and portfolio managers usually thwarts the model. The growth rates plugged into the model tend to be changed (in the wrong direction) at important turning points. Analysts become more bullish on a company's growth prospects when it is doing well and the stock is high. They are more pessimistic on future prospects after earnings decline and the stock is low. These changes in growth assumptions make overvalued stocks more attractive and cheap stocks more expensive—and usually at the wrong time.

COMPARISON OF RDY WITH OTHER INVESTMENT METHODS

It would be silly to suggest that RDY—or value investing, for that matter—is the *only* approach to equity investing. Relative Dividend Yield offers a conservative approach to the equity markets that has provided above-market returns with below-market risk. A few other approaches are described next that may be of more interest to institutional or individual investors. These approaches may fill their particular needs better than the RDY method. If this is the case, at least you don't have to read the rest of the book and I have saved you a lot of time!

Venture Capital

Getting in on "the ground floor," usually of a high-technology company, makes the venture capital approach the highest reward/ highest risk type of equity investing. It is for those seeking thrills, for those who do not need current income from their investments, and for those who can accept a low batting average, knowing that they will hit home runs the very few times they do connect.

Emerging Growth

This approach uses publicly traded stocks with some track record. It offers a higher batting average than does venture capital investing but with fewer home runs. In this approach, at least you know what the line up card looks like: These companies are usually thin on management, and their success is most often based on a narrow product line. These stocks are too popular in the marketplace most of the time. Typically, their stock prices cannot weather any disappointments. When bought on an "out-of-favor" valuation basis, they can be a very successful place to invest.

Looking at total market capitalization to annual revenues is a good valuation technique to use with these stocks. Low in current dividend income and generally unknown to the public, these companies are poorly covered by the large retail or institutional brokerage firms.

Large Growth

This approach is the most commonly followed by institutional investors and by many individuals as well. Many selection methods are used, most of them aimed at avoiding problems and being safe. Earnings growth, price momentum, earnings estimate changes, earnings surprises, and technical patterns have all been used with some success—and with even greater failure. Which stocks are cheap and which are expensive are more important here than with venture capital and emerging growth investing, where valuation is much more difficult and far less precise. Many institutional investors, both domestic and foreign, have portfolios of large-growth companies but lack a disciplined approach to their selection. These portfolios are often just a bunch of stocks put together without a theme or discipline.

Technical Analysis

Many technical approaches sound good on paper or are obvious after the fact. It is easy to see a declining trend once it is in place. At the turning points, when it is really important to make decisions, however, the technicians make a 50:50 bet. To repeat, reporting on the past is *not* a way to make money in the future.

Sector Rotators

Just as it is difficult—and debilitating to your wealth—to rely on short-term company earnings forecasts, it is even harder to analyze the quarterly and monthly variations in the reported economic data to predict which industry sectors will be next in favor. Trying to guess what the trends will be, let alone how the stock market will react to the data, has never proved to be a rewarding, long-term exercise. While it is useful to all investors to have some knowledge of where we are likely to be in a recession–recovery–boom cycle, trying to guess when each phase will end is neither necessary nor useful in the application of a disciplined, long-term approach. Sector rotators relying on a top-down economic approach have some of the most volatile and least successful long-term records in the investment business.

This does not mean that various industries or segments of the economy should not increase and decrease radically as a percent of a portfolio over a period of time. Indeed, as stocks go from being

28

cheap to being expensive using RDY, they should be added to and then removed from the portfolio. The point is that basing these changes on anticipating the economy rather than on identifying the value of stocks or an industry has not worked for very many investment managers.

3

AN RDY STUDY:
100 LARGE COMPANIES
FROM 1976 TO 1986

RDY RESEARCH

Just so that the RDY process does not seem too mysterious, or before you think that it requires too much time, talent, or staff to implement, let's look at the results generated simply by applying some basic statistics and investment decision rules.

The following research employed a similar approach to that developed for the study of dividend yield and yield change found in Appendix B. That study was presented at the Institute for Quantitative Analysis (Q Group) in the fall of 1990. But, rather than looking at 1500 stocks as in that study or even at 500 stocks, we constructed the following decision process.

We started with all of the stocks in the S&P 500 at the end of 1990 as our data base. In order to study a ten-year period, we began with 1976 and ended with 1986. (The year 1986 is the final date that could be used given the desire to test a four-year holding period, which proved to be the most effective holding period in the Q Group presentation—see Appendix B.) Any stocks for which data were incomplete for the period from 1976 to 1990 were removed. Also removed were all of the stocks that did not pay any dividends during the entire period since they would have always had a 0% RDY and a 0% RDY change.

Of the stocks that remained, we then selected the 100 largest companies based on market capitalizations as of each of the year-end periods from 1976 to 1986 and obtained 11 different portfolios. *Note:* International companies such as Royal Dutch and Unilever could not be used because the dividend does not have the same relationship to basic earnings power that it has for most of the major U.S.-headquartered companies. In addition, they do not pay dividends on a quarterly basis, which makes reliability of dividends more tenuous.

Table 3-1 shows the total return for all of the 100-stock portfolios. Included are the total returns for the S&P 500 and the 100 largest stocks for each four-year holding period beginning in 1976. The difference between the two groups is indicated in the last column. The results show that the *average* 100-largest-stocks portfolio (held for four years) beginning in 1976 returned 4.9% worse than the capitalization-weighted S&P 500.

These 100 largest stocks accounted for between 50% and 60% of

TABLE 3-1

Total Return for S&P 500 Versus 100 Largest Stocks

Year	S&P 500	100 largest	Difference
1976	47.6%	41.7%	−5.9%
1977	54.6%	49.8%	−4.8%
1978	73.3%	68.0%	−5.3%
1979	77.9%	76.5%	−1.4%
1980	44.3%	49.6%	5.3%
1981	96.8%	87.5%	−9.3%
1982	94.4%	88.7%	−5.7%
1983	69.8%	60.1%	−9.7%
1984	87.0%	77.8%	−9.2%
1985	85.5%	79.5%	−6.0%
1986	54.0%	51.7%	−2.3%
Average	**71.4%**	**66.4%**	**−4.9%**

the total value of the S&P 500 at the end of each year. The portfolios' dividend yields were very near those of the index itself, as shown in Table 3-2. They are a representative sample of the S&P 500. And yet, it is interesting to note that over this period, the equal-weighted 100 largest stocks did not perform as well as the capitalization-weighted S&P 500, as indicated in Table 3-1. It was not, as some would claim, a period when smaller-capitalization portfolio managers were at the mercy of the type of managers who use disciplines that rely on larger-capitalization, maturing companies.

We took the decision rules one step further for the 100-largest-stocks data base, employing what was done in the previous research work (Appendix B). Simply, our strategy was as follows:

- Buy the stocks with above-market yields (RDY above 100%) that *also* showed an increase in RDY from four years earlier.
- Hold the stocks for four years and then *sell*.

The use of RDY works on large companies with above-market yields and positive changes in RDY. Indeed, it was the group of

TABLE 3-2

Weighting and Yield of 100 Largest Stocks Relative to S&P 500

Year	100 Largest % of S&P		S&P 500 Index Yield
	Weighting	**Yield**	
1976	61.5	3.7	4.2
1977	59.7	4.7	5.5
1978	59.3	5.3	5.6
1979	56.9	5.3	5.5
1980	56.8	4.8	4.7
1981	53.4	5.4	5.5
1982	55.3	4.7	4.9
1983	54.7	4.1	4.4
1984	53.9	4.5	4.7
1985	54.2	4.0	3.8
1986	54.1	3.8	3.4

stocks with *both* above-market yields and positive RDY change that outperformed the universe of large companies and the market most significantly. The change in a company's RDY may come from either a change in dividend rate or a change in the stock price. As is discussed in more detail in Appendix B, the source of the movement in RDY change does not appear to make much difference. The critical factor is that the stock's yield rises to the area where it is historically compelling relative to the market. In the large majority of cases, of course, this happens due to a drop in the stock's price rather than to a dividend hike. It is the yield as an indicator of value that counts. If the yield has gone up, it does not matter why.

The use of RDY provided, along with an above-market income stream, excess total return and lower volatility of returns over the long term. Comparing the decision-rule results with average results from the same 100-stock universes at year-end (thereby eliminating the differences in results between the market and these same large companies) provided even higher excess returns.

Table 3-3 indicates the average excess return achieved over the

TABLE 3-3

Excess Return Based on 100 Largest Stocks (Equally Weighted)

	RDY Change	
RDY Levels	**Four-Year Increase in RDY**	**Four-Year Decrease in RDY**
Above market	**10.3%**	−5.1%
Below market	−4.2%	−4.9%

entire period from 1976 to 1986 using the stock selection method previously outlined. Using this simple discipline, knowing nothing else about the companies, and consulting no RDY charts, an investor would have outperformed the 100-largest-stocks data base. Moreover, it should be noted that these results include the year 1990, a very bad year for high-yield stocks. Thus, if the study had used data only through 1989, the excess returns would have been considerably higher.

Table 3-4 reviews the results for the 11 portfolios from year-end 1976 to 1986. Just looking at high absolute yield alone, as shown in Table 3-5, or at the positive four-year change in RDY alone, as shown in Table 3-6, did not generate excess returns (versus the 100-

TABLE 3-4

Total Returns for Following Four Years Based on Both RDY above 100% and Previous Four-Year Change

	RDY Change	
RDY Levels	**Four-Year Increase in RDY**	**Four-Year Decrease in RDY**
Above market	**76.7%**	61.4%
Below market	62.2%	61.6%

TABLE 3-5

Excess Return Based on Yield Level Alone

RDY Levels	Total Return	Excess Return vs.	
		100 Largest	S&P 500
Above market	73.1%	−6.6%	+1.7%
Below market	61.0%	−5.5%	−10.4%

largest-stocks universe or the market) nearly as high as did looking at both factors together. Using RDY and RDY change provided an average excess return over the 100-largest-stocks universe of 10.3%.

TABLE 3-6

Excess Return Based on Yield Change Alone

RDY Change	Total Return	Excess Return vs.	
		100 Largest	S&P 500
Four-year increase	68.8%	+2.3%	−2.6%
Four-year decrease	60.0%	−6.5%	+11.4%

WHAT CAN GO WRONG WITH THESE RULES

From a purely mechanical point of view, some stocks will take longer than the four years to reach their potential while others will achieve their performance more rapidly, become overvalued, and decline again all in the space of a four-year period. Stocks also may have started from such an undervalued level (very high RDY) that even a sharp decline in RDY over a four-year period will still place them in "cheap" territory in terms of RDY and they should *not* have been sold. While this mechanistic approach works, reviewing the RDY charts in Appendix C or plotting your own charts on stocks of interest gives a better idea most of the time of under- and overvaluation levels than does a specific, predefined time period.

While a portfolio of stocks with the characteristics of an RDY above the market and an increase in RDY from four years earlier does not provide better returns than the market or the 100 largest stocks each and every year, it is an effective way of achieving higher total returns over the long term. Most institutional investors and many individual investors use large-company stocks in their portfolios, and applying the RDY approach will provide them with a decision rule that works with discipline and patience.

4

THE RDY APPROACH IN PRACTICE

HOW RDY HAS WORKED AND WHY

In case there is still any confusion, a stock's yield is its current annual dividend divided by its current price. For example, a stock that has a market price of $20 and that pays a $1 dividend would have a 5% dividend yield. As has already been pointed out, RDY works on current dividends and dividend yields; *no forecasts of future dividends are involved.* The stock's current dividend yield is the starting point.

High yield alone, however, is not enough. As discussed briefly in the previous chapters, the RDY investor also considers a stock's yield relative to the market's yield. It is not unusual for analysts or other investors to say, "XYZ stock looks really attractive. It's selling at a 5% yield." But, how do you know whether it is "really attractive" without knowing the overall market's yield? If the market were yielding 6%, for example, then 5% would not be as attractive as it is when the market's yield is at the 4% level.

Nor is yield relative to the market sufficient. The RDY investor compares a stock's yield not only with the market's yield but also with its own yield over time. This factor also differentiates the RDY approach from other yield-based styles.

What we are really considering is *historical* RDY. Just as a stock is not attractive using this approach until its yield is higher than the market's yield, it also is not attractive until its yield reaches the buy range established by the stock's own unique RDY history.

Consider what a difference historical RDY makes when you look at utility stocks. A utility stock will probably always provide a yield that is at a premium to the market's, but this premium must enter the stock's own historical RDY buy range before we are interested in buying it. High absolute yield alone is not enough!

When you examine companies' RDYs over time, many stocks show a repetitive pattern. The RDY investor is interested in buying high—buying when the stock is at the upper end of its historical RDY range—and selling low—selling when the stock is at the lower end of its historical RDY range. Consider, again, the example of the XYZ Corporation that was discussed in Chapter 1.

As shown here in Figure 4-1, when the stock falls out of favor— when most investors are simply not interested in the stock—the

FIGURE 4-1

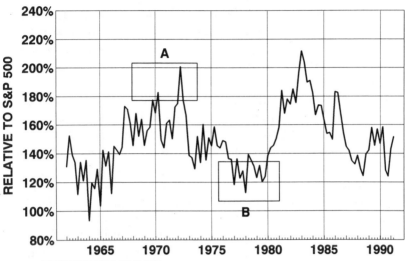

XYZ Corporation, Relative Dividend Yield, 1962–1991

QUARTERLY OBSERVATIONS ARE IN JAN, APR, JUL & OCT

price falls, the yield goes up, and the stock enters an attractive buy range ("A"). Later, when everybody discovers some important factors that bring the company back into favor, the yield drops relative to the market and the stock enters the sell part of the range ("B"). In the interim, the investor has been paid a market premium (in terms of yield) to wait for the company's prospects to change and, therefore, locks in a healthy capital gain. The RDY is a powerful indicator of under- and overvaluation.

The candidates to consider when using RDY are large, maturing companies, generally those with household names. Investors who use RDY start with an advantage: They need not look at thousands of companies. All stocks that do not have above-market yields are eliminated. Over 200 stocks have been candidates at some point during the past ten years. Usually, fewer than 100 stocks are of interest at any one point in time. Appendix C contains the historical RDY graphs for a number of candidates, many of which are attractive now or may be attractive again during the next ten years.

As the Dow-Jones study detailed in Appendix A and the work

discussed in the previous chapter indicate, extensive research is not necessary to produce competitive returns. Future chapters will discuss how research keeps the investor from making painful mistakes and introduces new ideas that can be very successful. *Note: Although the authors' firm of Spare, Tengler, Kaplan, and Bischel uses research from its analysts, it is because of their understanding of the RDY discipline and years of experience that their work helps in the portfolio management process.*

Stock selection and dividend analysis will be discussed in a later chapter. For now, in order to discuss the RDY process in depth, we will assume that the investor already has a universe of qualified stocks—large, maturing companies with dividend yields above the market's yield.

As indicated in the short introduction to RDY in Chapter 1, the market yield used for various comparisons in this book is the yield of the S&P 500. It does not matter which index is selected since the buy and sell ranges merely shift. If you were using the S&P 400 stock universe, 1.40 times market yield would be about the same as 1.25 times the yield of the S&P 500. Over the last 30 years, the S&P 500 has provided a yield roughly 10% higher than that of the S&P 400. It makes no difference to the RDY discipline. The investor could use the DJIA or almost any market benchmark. Studies have shown that the results are comparable.

THE BASIC PROCESS: SETTING THE RDY RANGES

Without experience accumulated over time, setting the proper RDY ranges can seem like a most difficult task. It is important to point out that great precision is *not* required. One of the powerful features of RDY investing is that the use of RDY illuminates broad ranges of under- and overvaluation. Success does not rely on either split-second timing in the implementation of the RDY approach or a single magic point of purchase or sale. It is more important to be roughly right than precisely wrong. Timing and staging in the implementation process can greatly enhance total return, but as demonstrated in Chapter 3, a mechanical approach will still produce well above market returns.

On some stocks, the appropriate ranges jump out. Those stocks that have had a reasonably repetitive pattern over the years are the easiest on which to set the ranges. Stocks, like the oil group, over the last 30 years, have experienced the cyclical emotionalism captured so well by the RDY approach. As long as the beginning buy level and beginning sell level are set at least 20% apart to avoid unnecessary transactions and turnover, the exact levels are not important.

Dealing with "Fallen Angels"

Since the so-called fallen-angel growth stocks have no past history as income stocks, they have no pattern of RDY upon which to rely. First of all, remember that RDY works only on the stocks of large companies that have above-market yields. As a simple rule of thumb, begin buying this type of stock when 10% higher than a market (S&P 500) yield is reached. Wait and watch. See whether the yield continues to move significantly upward before adding to or finishing investment positions. If the yield relative to the market does not move much beyond the market, the worst that can happen is that you do not own as much of a really great investment as you want. If the RDY does continue to increase, at least you have the chance to dollar-cost-average with lower prices. Without any history, start reducing the stock's position when it reaches 0.90 of the market's yield and eliminate it when it reaches 0.75 (three-quarters) of the market's yield. If there is continued growth in dividends above the rate of the market, the stock will continue to advance after it has been sold. Just because a stock's yield reaches well below the market's yield does not mean that the stock will stop doing well, but for the RDY investor the yield is no longer high enough to justify ownership.

Over time, there may be reason to adjust these ranges upward as the particular company increases in size and as the growth of earnings slows with increased maturity. For many of the fallen-angel growth stocks, however, there is not a repetitive chance to buy, sell, and buy back again, even within a five- to ten-year period. Included in Appendix C are several stocks of this type that were cheap using RDY in the early 1980s and that may become cheap again by the mid-1990s. Eli Lilly, Coca-Cola, Boeing, and Procter & Gamble all fall into the category of stocks that were cheap but that have not become cheap again during the past seven to eight years. Keep watching, however, because the prospects may change!

Dealing with Cyclicals

The stocks most difficult to set ranges on are the very mature cyclical stocks. The risk of dividend cuts is the greatest on these stocks and makes the pattern of RDY less reliable as the sole indicator of emotion that can be used in a contrary manner. However, compared with most other valuation techniques, RDY is by far a superior tool to use in reviewing these stocks in spite of the potential risk of dividend cuts. There are signs the investor can watch out for when dividend-cut risk is of concern (see Chapter 6).

The idea of the RDY approach is to look at the difference between the average selling prices and the average purchase prices. If the selling price is high enough above the average buying price to generate an above-average return when adding back the dividend collected each quarter, then the investment has been successful. There is a virtual certainty that this approach will not result in buying all the shares at an absolute low in price. There is the same guarantee that the investor will not sell all shares at the high. But, if the discipline is followed, the RDY investor will enjoy significant capital appreciation *and* dividend income.

Measuring Attractiveness

The application of RDY is a very useful way of separating the emotionalism of investors from the reality of the specific company's fundamentals. One of the warning signs indicating that a further look at the safety of the dividend may be needed occurs when the RDY is very high and the change in RDY from four years before is much greater than that of other stocks:

44

	Increase in RDY	Very Large Increase in RDY
Far-above-market yield	High, but . . . . A very high yield, but has been there before.	Watch out! A very high yield is unusual, particularly when increased so much from four years before.
Above-market yield	"Goldie Locks" Just about right—above-market yield and cheaper than before.	Very expensive before? A large change in RDY from four years before may indicate that the stock was very expensive before.

Let's consider an easy example first. We begin by looking at the stock's unique RDY history as far back as possible. Refer to Figure 4-2.

Usually, a meaningful pattern emerges in RDY charts. The particular company of Figure 4-2, the so-called ABC Corporation, has experienced very definite periods of over- and undervaluation during the last 30 years. The RDY history for this stock contains much information.

After looking at the RDY history, the next step is to establish buy and sell ranges. Based on history, where is a good place to at least begin looking at this company as a potential purchase? Studying RDY charts is the best way to develop an understanding and a "feel" for setting the appropriate buy and sell ranges. One of the great advantages of RDY is that investors do not have to establish the exact time or price at which a stock is at its absolute cheapest—the point when it will decline no further. Very few investors have a history of identifying this single point of time or price. RDY is implemented successfully using *ranges*. A beginning point to the buy range provides the investor with a perspective on the stock's cheapness and an opportunity to scale into a position over time—often averaging the total cost down. The same, of course, would be true in reverse for establishing the sell range.

The same RDY chart as shown in Figure 4-2 is repeated in

45

FIGURE 4-2

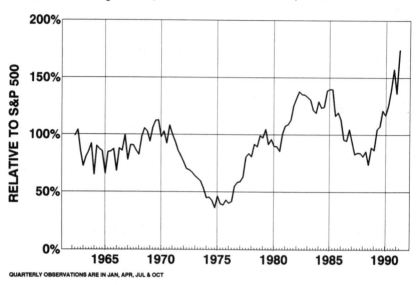

ABC Corporation, Relative Dividend Yield, 1962–1991

QUARTERLY OBSERVATIONS ARE IN JAN, APR, JUL & OCT

Figure 4-3, this time with RDY buy and sell ranges suggested. Looking at this chart adds the final perspective required for the investor to make a timely and well-informed decision. The stock was a buy when the yield rose above the top bar, from 1982 to 1985, and a sell when the yield fell below the bottom bar, in late 1987.

There is no magic to setting ranges. We use experience and opinion to help us determine where the ranges should be based on the stock's own history. In most instances, the buy and sell ranges are apparent when you look at a chart of a stock's RDY history.

The exceptions are the fallen-angel growth stocks, such as IBM and Xerox (see Figure 4-4), whose long-term RDY history offers no recurrent pattern. Until recently, during the last ten years, Xerox had a yield consistently far below that of the market. However, buying opportunities did occur in this stock in recent years.

When the yield of a fallen-angel growth stock reaches a level where the RDY investor is interested, it helps to look at analogous stocks—in this case, Du Pont or General Motors—that were also

FIGURE 4-3

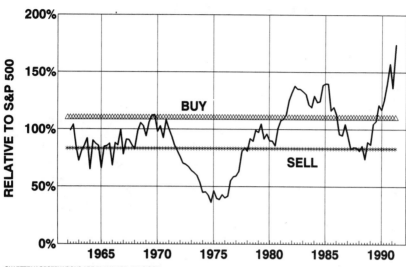

ABC Corporation, Relative Dividend Yield, 1962–1991,
Marked Buy and Sell

FIGURE 4-4

Xerox, Relative Dividend Yield, 1962–1991

FIGURE 4-5

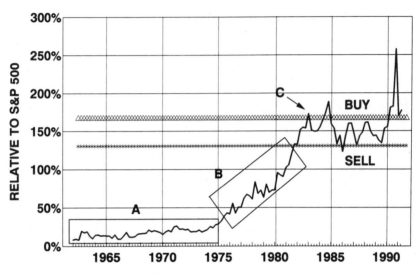

Xerox, Relative Dividend Yield, 1962–1991

QUARTERLY OBSERVATIONS ARE IN JAN, APR, JUL & OCT

growth stocks for decades until they, too, became maturing companies. But, their maturation began years ago, well before it happened to Xerox. Setting the buy range (see Figure 4-5) at point "C," when the stock has gone from stage "A" through transition stage "B" to the point of complete disappointment and neglect, takes courage and knowledge of analogous situations. When it comes time to consider buying according to the range that has been established, we add in company and market knowledge to determine whether we do, in fact, take a position—and how much of a position—at this particular time in the stock's history. However, RDY does not require this knowledge to generate excess returns. (Portfolio construction is discussed in more detail in a later chapter.)

GROUPING THE STOCKS

There are many ways that any list of stocks can be organized. We prefer to divide stocks into broad economic sectors and will discuss individual issues in this context later. Included are some past successes as well as some current ideas and a few problem issues.

Another way to look at stocks is by broad types: traditional income stocks, cyclicals, and the so-called fallen-angel growth stocks.

The traditional high-yield stocks are usually in the slow-growth industries for which investors, expecting little in the way of earnings growth, demand to be paid a large portion of their return in the form of current dividends. The use of RDY does not force the investor to own *only* this group as absolute-yield investing may, but it does lead the investor to this group of stocks when they are most attractive. Examples of traditional yield stocks include electric utilities, telephone companies, natural gas companies, some banks, and some insurance companies when their yields are high relative to their past histories. They are not bought on the basis of high absolute yields, the basis used by most yield investors, but only when their dividend yields are particularly high relative to the market and their own history.

Cyclicals, stocks that present problems to low P/E investors if a company's earnings are down, are handled well by looking at RDY. A stock's P/E may be high when earnings are depressed and look unattractive on this basis. If the dividend has been maintained, however, the RDY is likely to be high as well, and the stock will be attractive on this basis. The P/E does not matter.

The previously discussed fallen-angel growth stocks are a third broad group. The ability of the RDY approach to use this type of issue differentiates it from the approaches of most traditional value/yield buyers. This group of stocks has long been viewed by investors as consisting of growth stocks that have either matured to the point where growth has slowed or that have had some disappointing quarterly earnings. Whatever the reason, their drop in earnings has prompted growth investors to dump these stocks and *neglect* them. When the dividend is maintained by boards of directors who believe earnings problems are temporary, and the dividend is sustainable even with disappointing earnings, their dividend yield rises to a level that is very high relative to the market's yield and the companies' past histories. They can be very attractive buys for the RDY investor.

The fallen-angel growth stocks, shunned by disillusioned growth investors and seldom considered by traditional high-yield investors, fall between the cracks into a "no man's land." These stocks' yields are high relative to their own past, but they still do not provide absolute yields as high as, say, the traditional yield stocks. In this inefficient sector of the market, RDY investors can find some of their best investments. Some of the most interesting and profitable stocks have been fallen-angel growth stocks.

The scale of attractiveness and unattractiveness is different for each type of stock. Fallen-angel growth stocks, as just noted, are very different in terms of valuation levels from electric utility companies. A utility's yield may have to be more than twice the market's yield before the RDY investor is interested; a fallen angel can be worth looking at when its yield is only slightly above the market's yield.

Companies can, over time, move from one of the three categories of stocks into another. Any company whose unit growth has begun to slow will quickly qualify as a cyclical or even, eventually, as a high-yield stock, and there can be reversals of this pattern. Food industry stocks, for example, in the late 1970s were considered yield stocks in the traditional sense; they are now thought of as growth stocks. In time, they may revert to yield-stock status again. Are Kellogg and Campbell Soup really growth stocks? Back in the late 1970s, they experienced 2% to 3% unit growth at a time when inflation was rampant and they could not raise their prices fast enough to cover higher costs. Electric utilities, a group that in many investors' professional memory has always consisted of yield stocks, were actually considered growth companies in the 1950s and 1960s. And, have the telephone utilities not been looked at as growth stocks by many investors in recent years? The stocks were at historical RDY lows and showed up in many growth portfolios near the end of 1989 just before a period of earnings disappointment and price decline.

Another interesting example is the tobacco industry. In the late 1960s and early 1970s, it was considered a growth industry. The price of the stocks—Philip Morris is a prime example—rose tremendously and pushed yields down to about half that of the market. Philip Morris, as will be discussed in Chapter 5, traded at a

50

half-of-market yield range for a very long time. Then, suddenly, in the 1980s, the tobacco industry, under attack from all sides, became highly suspect; not only were they not a growth industry anymore, but it was feared that they might experience a downturn in earnings. Worried investors wanted nothing to do with tobacco stocks. The RDY of Philip Morris was pushed up to well over any level that it had been before, except for the early 1960s, creating a prime buying opportunity for the RDY investor. The stock did not stay at a high RDY and depressed-price level for very long and has since gone on to be a very strong performer in recent years.

In summary, three kinds of stocks are available to the RDY investor: traditional-yield stocks, cyclicals, and fallen-angel growth stocks. Individual stocks and even industries can move within these three groups over time. Relative Dividend Yield provides a tool for investing in each of these types of stocks by identifying when they are "cheap" and when they are "dear."

Let's consider three examples in detail. The practical use of RDY in three very different industries—energy, photography, and food—should prove to be very informative.

RDY IN PRACTICE: SOME EXAMPLES

The discussion of earnings and other company, as well as industry, factors in the following examples provides an understanding of the environment within which RDY is generated. This is not information that must be analyzed to own a portfolio of high-yield stocks that will do well with lower-than-market risk. Clearly, for those readers with the time and resources to look at balance sheets, cash flows, and earnings, the risks to the dividend payment can be analyzed. Included later is a section that discusses the various techniques of fundamental securities analysis that have been applied. With research, the big RDY mistakes—buying a stock with high odds of a dividend cut or omission—can be minimized. This analysis will enhance the use of RDY, but it is not necessary in order to arrive at a different view from that held by most investors of a stock's valuation.

Energy Industry Example

Chevron.   Chevron is an excellent example of how RDY can be used as a signal of when to buy and when to sell. Dividends are powerful indicators of how management and a board of directors feel about their company for the long term. They provide re-assurance to investors when fears about the company's future earnings are high, and they dampen enthusiasm when optimism has been exaggerated.

Like most other companies in the petroleum business, Chevron's RDY charts, as shown in Figures 4-6 and 4-7, show wide swings in investor enthusiasm and despair. The expectations by analysts, economists, and investors for oil prices have swung over the past 20 years from $2/bbl in 1973 ("A"), to $60/bbl in 1980 ("B"), to $5/bbl in 1986 ("C"), and back to $50/bbl in 1990 ("D"). The psychology of investors has gone from the viewpoint of asking, "Why own these stocks—they are just self-liquidating bonds?" to

FIGURE 4-6

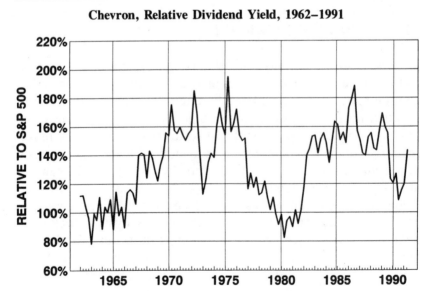

Chevron, Relative Dividend Yield, 1962–1991

QUARTERLY OBSERVATIONS ARE IN JAN, APR, JUL & OCT

FIGURE 4-7

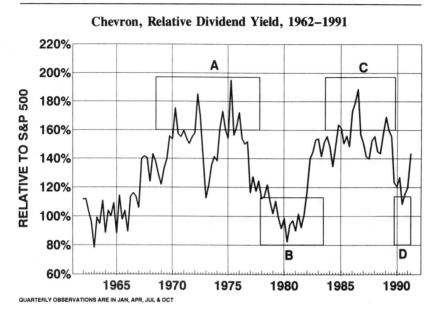

Chevron, Relative Dividend Yield, 1962–1991

QUARTERLY OBSERVATIONS ARE IN JAN, APR, JUL & OCT

suggesting, "They are great growth companies and inflation hedges—stocks for all times and markets." Like most things, the truth lies somewhere between the extremes.

When looked at in terms of the market, Chevron and most of the other oil issues have been quite volatile, reflecting the cyclical nature of the industry as well as the external and unpredictable events that affect their future prospects. Looking carefully at Chevron shows the problems that arise with the more traditional methods of valuation.

Figure 4-8 shows the per share dividends and earnings history of Chevron from the start of 1962 to the end of 1990. The earnings have been cyclical, but the dividend has risen consistently over the last 29 years. The treatment of the dividend in the late 1970s, which rose much more slowly than the explosive earnings expansion, indicates the management's care and conservatism in setting the dividend rate.

Figure 4-9 shows the price/earnings multiple of Chevron from 1962 to the end of 1990. As with most cyclical stocks, the P/E is very

FIGURE 4-8

Chevron, Per Share Dividends and Earnings, 1962–1991

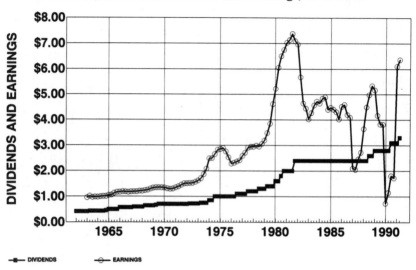

QUARTERLY OBSERVATIONS ARE IN JAN, APR, JUL & OCT

FIGURE 4-9

Chevron, Price/Earnings Multiple, 1962–1991

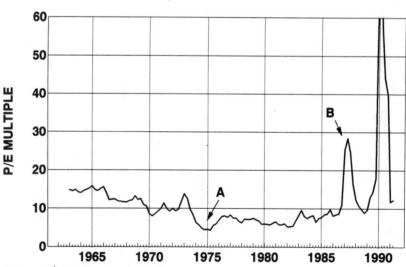

QUARTERLY OBSERVATIONS ARE IN JAN, APR, JUL & OCT

high when earnings are depressed and very low at the times of peak earnings. The multiple was less than 5 times earnings during period "A" and rose beyond 20 times during period "B." Buying when the P/E is low and selling when P/Es are high just does not work with cyclical stocks like Chevron. For example, when earnings were depressed in 1986, the P/E was very high, but the price reached a bottom relative to the market.

Again, Figures 4-6 and 4-7 show the RDY for the company. Figure 4-10 shows the RDY and relative price. Very clear periods of "cheapness" and "dearness" have occurred, as reflected in the RDY. Chevron was cheap for most of the mid-1970s when you look at RDY ("A"), and the stock proceeded to advance sharply ("B"). By the mid-1980s, the stock looked very cheap again ("C"). Based on RDY, Chevron has been expensive when the yield was below the market's yield. For some companies and industries, yield above the market is the norm, while, for others, yield below the market is more usual. Since the oil industry is mature, it is characterized by

FIGURE 4-10

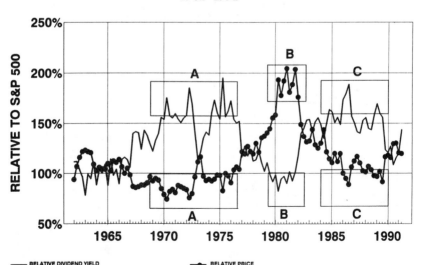

Chevron, Relative Dividend Yield and Relative Price, 1962–1991

QUARTERLY OBSERVATIONS ARE IN JAN, APR, JUL & OCT

Price Index 12/86 = 100

55

lower-earnings-growth prospects and above-market yields except during periods of extreme oil shortage and crisis.

While Chevron stayed expensive for many months in the early 1980s, the overvaluation was eventually rectified with the collapse in share price. Table 4-1 shows that from a month-end price of $58 at the peak in the oil mania during November of 1980, Chevron fell to $25 by the end of July of 1982—a decline of 57%—while the S&P 500 declined only 24%, from $141 to $107. Chevron's low price relative to the S&P 500, however, did not occur until 1986. During the four years from July of 1982 to July of 1986, Chevron rose 44% to $36, but the S&P 500 jumped 120% to $236. By 1986, investors had again dumped the stock and the RDY was at very high levels, just before another period of strong advance.

Table 4-1 shows the price changes for Chevron during various periods of time. In addition to the price changes, however, remember that the dividend stream is a key part of total return on an investment and is not included in this comparison.

Looking back at Figure 4-8, it is important to note that when earnings increased threefold during the second half of the 1970s, the dividend only doubled. Management did not trust the sustainability of the earnings being reported at the time. By the mid-1980s, when earnings per share fell below the dividend, management's confidence in a return to higher earnings levels from 1986's depressed levels was reflected in a decision to maintain their

TABLE 4-1

Chevron RDY and Price Performance

| Month End | Chevron | | | S&P 500 | |
	RDY	Price	% Change	Price	% Change
Jul 1974	170%	$13		$79	
Nov 1980	80%	$58	346%	$141	78%
Jul 1982	150%	$25	−57%	$107	−24%
Jul 1986	190%	$36	44%	$236	120%
Jul 1990	110%	$79	119%	$356	50%

dividend rate despite the earnings decline. In short, *the dividend reflects management's view of a portion of normal, sustainable earnings.*

Photographic Business Example

Eastman Kodak. As the leading company in the photographic business, Eastman Kodak was one of the great growth companies in the United States and the world. Kodak's success was a result of the improving standard of living throughout the world after World War II. The company experienced very rapid earnings growth until the mid-1970s and was valued in the marketplace as a premier growth company. From the early 1960s to the peak of the Nifty Fifty growth-stock mania in 1973, Eastman Kodak's stock price advanced at a pace 3.5 times that of the market. Its yield for this period in the company's history averaged about half of the market's yield, below 3%, as can be seen in Figure 4-11.

FIGURE 4-11

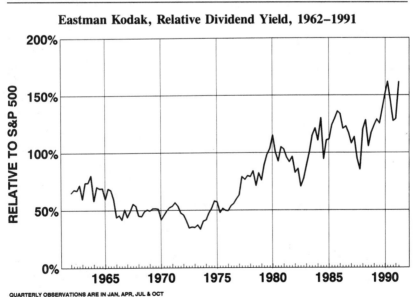

Eastman Kodak, Relative Dividend Yield, 1962–1991

QUARTERLY OBSERVATIONS ARE IN JAN, APR, JUL & OCT

With the start of an escalation in silver, chemicals, and packaging prices in the mid-1970s, Kodak's earnings fell below the investment community's expectations. Kodak's RDY rose from less than 50% to more than 160% of the market's yield (see Figure 4-12, period "A" to "C"). The absolute yield went from below 2% in the 1960s and early 1970s to over 6% in early 1980. The RDY was above 100% of the market's yield throughout the 1980s, except for short periods from 1981 to 1983 (period "B"). The RDY was still low in 1980 and reached a peak (at point "C") in 1990, when the absolute yield was about 5%.

Kodak has been out of investment favor for most of the past decade. The earnings growth slowed dramatically, and then the acquisition of Sterling Drug in 1988 caused investor concern about Kodak's future growth as the balance sheet bloated with debt. By the time Polaroid's antitrust settlement was announced in 1990, Kodak's RDY exceeded 60% above the S&P 500's yield.

Kodak's reported earnings, as indicated in Figure 4-13, have

FIGURE 4-12

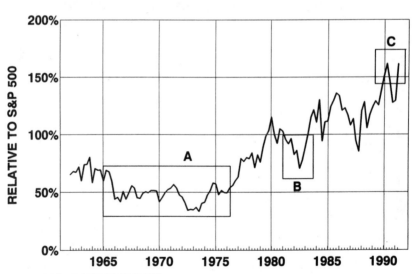

Eastman Kodak, Relative Dividend Yield, 1962–1991

QUARTERLY OBSERVATIONS ARE IN JAN, APR, JUL & OCT

FIGURE 4-13

Eastman Kodak, Per Share Dividends and Earnings, 1962–1991

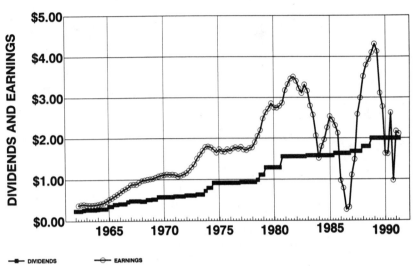

QUARTERLY OBSERVATIONS ARE IN JAN, APR, JUL & OCT

been very volatile in the last five years, but the dividend has increased steadily. Figure 4-14 shows the reported price/earnings multiple. A P/E of about 50 times earnings was reached in 1972 (period "A") when Kodak was a market favorite. Despite the decline in share price from $65 to $40 from 1972 to 1990, the P/E reached nearly 50 times earnings (period "B") again—this time, not because Eastman Kodak was a market favorite, but because its earnings per share declined. The period of very low profits in 1986 caused the stock's P/E to approach 150 times earnings (period "C"). Once again, note how the investor can be misled using P/Es as a measure of value or "cheapness."

Kodak has revised its growth expectations downward, giving it better potential for positive future earnings surprises. It has embarked on plant closings, early retirement programs, and other cost-reduction programs, all of which have impacted earnings negatively, but which should help future earnings. Given the high RDY level, investment community expectations do not yet reflect these

FIGURE 4-14

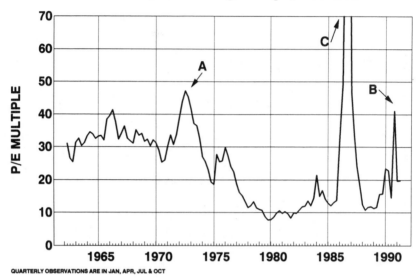

Eastman Kodak, Price/Earnings Multiple, 1962–1991

QUARTERLY OBSERVATIONS ARE IN JAN, APR, JUL & OCT

programs' benefits but are still extrapolating the most recent period of earnings problems.

Food Industry Example

Kellogg. The consumer food industry was hard hit by the increase in ingredient costs during the 1970s and the increased market share achieved by private-label brands. The rather steady pace of annual earnings advances typical of nondurable branded goods paled relative to the sharp advances being experienced by the industrial, commodity, and technology sectors of the economy during the late 1970s' inflationary boom. The food stocks went from being among the market favorites of the 1950s and early 1960s to a position of neglect in the early 1980s.

The early 1980s brought lower inflation and market share gains for national-branded goods and lower ingredient and packaging costs for the food industry. At the same time, there were earnings

60

disappointments in the basic industry and industrial segments of the economy that had been strong in the 1970s. During most of the 1980s, the food stocks again became the great growth favorites of the investment markets. Because of the stability of their cash flows, many of these companies became targets for acquisitions and leveraged buy-outs. In response, many food industry firms restructured their balance sheets with higher debt and repurchased their shares to absorb the potential supply of the shares outstanding. This increased reported earnings-per-share growth rates and led to renewed investor enthusiasm not seen since the early 1960s. The food stocks went from their neglected position to become "darlings," and their stock prices rose sharply.

A prime example is Kellogg, a leader in the ready-to-eat cold cereal business. Its stock has experienced a roller coaster performance, as volatile as any company in the food industry. Ups and downs in terms of growth, neglect, and excitement are all in evidence when you look at its RDY chart (see Figure 4-15). The pressure on margins and the below-average relative growth rate for

FIGURE 4-15

Kellogg, Relative Dividend Yield, 1962–1991

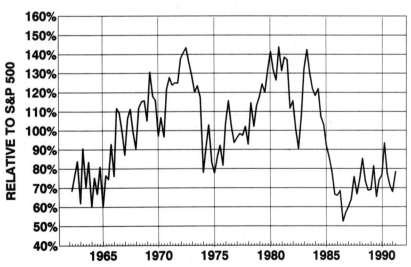

QUARTERLY OBSERVATIONS ARE IN JAN, APR, JUL & OCT

Kellogg in the late 1970s were the basic causes of Kellogg's yield exceeding 7% when the S&P 500 yield was below 6%. After many years of annual earnings growth above 15% a year in the mid-1970s, earnings growth slowed as inflationary pressures reduced margins. An RDY of 140%, or a 40% premium above the market, was reached during 1981.

After several years of downwardly revised expectations leading to the opportunity for positive surprises, Kellogg became a market favorite again in 1985, as indicated by its RDY. From its relative high in 1981, Kellogg's absolute dividend yield dropped to about 1.5% in 1986, or a relative yield only 50% of the S&P 500 yield of 3%.

The emotional level of the investor community is reflected in a stock's RDY history. Just as all of the preceding examples discussed the environment of growth and profit expectations, the same is done here for Kellogg to elucidate how this type of background information is likely to become the basis of common parlance when stocks are either at a point of "cheapness" or "expensiveness."

Using dividend yield relative to the market as a valuation technique simply works better than using price/earnings ratios or absolute yield. Figure 4-16 for Kellogg shows the history of this former fallen-angel growth stock. Dividends have not declined over the last 30 years, and earnings have been higher than dividends all the time. Reported earnings dipped in 1989 due to nonrecurring write-offs, but operating earnings continued to advance. Despite this absence of earnings cyclicality, investor emotions about Kellogg's attractiveness as an investment continued to fluctuate markedly.

Figure 4-17 shows that the stock did about the same as the S&P 500 during the 1960s and early 1970s (period "A"). A sharp rise in relative performance followed in the mid-1970s (period "B"). The stock, along with many other food and beverage stocks, then fell sharply. It bottomed in the early 1980s (period "C"), when very high levels of RDY indicated that it was undervalued by historical standards. Since then, Kellogg has been a superior performer in a strong market environment (period "D"). From January of 1984 to year-end 1990, Kellogg moved from $16 to $76. During the same time, the S&P 500 increased from $163 to $325. Kellogg's price

FIGURE 4-16

Kellogg, Per Share Dividends and Earnings, 1962–1991

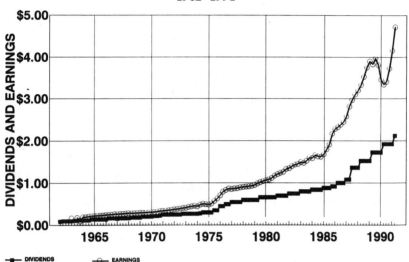

QUARTERLY OBSERVATIONS ARE IN JAN, APR, JUL & OCT

FIGURE 4-17

Kellogg, Relative Dividend Yield and Relative Price, 1962–1991

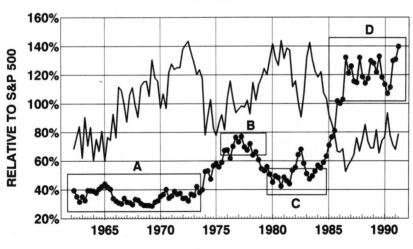

QUARTERLY OBSERVATIONS ARE IN JAN, APR, JUL & OCT   Price Index 12/86=100

FIGURE 4-18

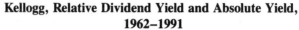

**Kellogg, Relative Dividend Yield and Absolute Yield,
1962–1991**

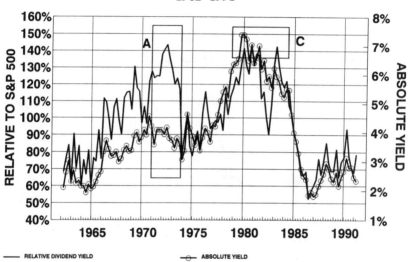

RELATIVE DIVIDEND YIELD   ABSOLUTE YIELD

QUARTERLY OBSERVATIONS ARE IN JAN, APR, JUL & OCT

increased 3.75 times since the RDY reached 140%, which compares favorably with a double in the overall market.

As can be seen in Figure 4-18, both absolute yield and RDY were high in the late 1970s and indicated Kellogg's cheapness during period "C." This was not true, however, in period "A." The high level of RDY indicated the attractiveness of the stock before the move to "B" on Figure 4-17, while absolute yield did not help.

These three examples are representative of the power of RDY as a valuation technique. There are more to follow. It is important to note that during periods of Wall Street pessimism and neglect, RDY provides the discipline to go against the crowd—a time-proven way to make money.

5

MORE EXAMPLES OF
RDY VALUATIONS

CONSUMER STOCKS

Food and Beverage

Coca-Cola. Coca-Cola has been one of the great worldwide growth investments for more than 50 years. No one would think that an income-oriented discipline would have any application for the stock of the leading soft-drink manufacturer. Indeed, Coca-Cola's growth has seldom been interrupted. In the 1970 to 1973 Nifty Fifty/Tier I growth-stock binge, Coca-Cola was selling at less than half of the market's yield of about 3% (see Figure 5-1, period "A").

Then, in the mid-1970s, problems arose. The price of sugar—a vital ingredient at that time—started to skyrocket. In less than two years, the price of this commodity went from 10 cents per pound to over 60 cents. By the late 1970s, container prices were also increasing sharply, and Coca-Cola's profit margins were under pressure. Furthermore, soft drink consumption had increased to the point where theories were appearing about the inability of the human body to ingest more soft drinks without adverse health consequences. Saturation of both the body and the marketplace was feared. The stock's RDY began to rise.

Perhaps worried that its growth potential was indeed threatened, Coca-Cola's management decided to diversify; it acquired the entertainment company Columbia Pictures. The first movie released in 1982 under the new ownership was "Annie," which proved to be an expensive flop.

Then, from 1974 to 1982, Coca-Cola's stock was under pressure. By the late 1970s, the stock had entered a transition period: Its earnings growth was slow enough to worry growth investors, and the yield was not high enough to attract income investors. Since Coca-Cola was a "growth" stock that was no longer growing, there was little interest in the company, and its shares continued to decline relative to the market. From 1974, when its RDY was less than 50% of the market's yield, to 1980, when the RDY exceeded 140% of the market's yield (Figure 5-1), Coca-Cola was a very poor stock to own in terms of both capital appreciation and relative

FIGURE 5-1

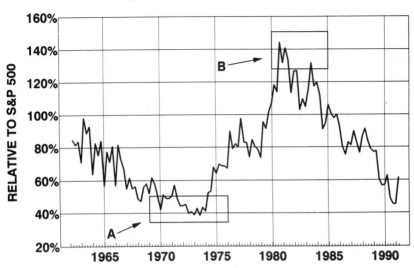

Coca-Cola, Relative Dividend Yield, 1962–1991

QUARTERLY OBSERVATIONS ARE IN JAN, APR, JUL & OCT

performance. This is indicated in Figure 5-1 from time period "A" to "B."

As indicated in Figure 5-2, however, the company's dividends and earnings have progressed steadily upward with few exceptions. When these exceptions occurred and earnings failed to advance, the market usually overreacted, which created further buying opportunities.

Since that low point in the early 1980s, when investors were concerned about the movie business and foresaw little growth in the soft drink business, the stock has risen for nearly a decade with few pauses. It stopped being attractive for income investors when the yield dropped below the market's yield in 1985, although the stock continued to advance strongly.

Over the last five years, Coca-Cola has once again become a growth-stock favorite as domestic and foreign sales have expanded and earnings have surged. The stock now sells at a yield of less than 2%, once again below half the market's yield. This RDY of 50% has not been seen since 1974—the euphoric period of popularity

67

FIGURE 5-2

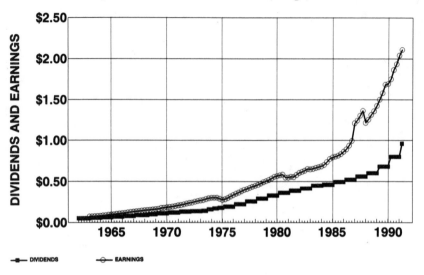

Coca-Cola, Per Share Dividends and Earnings, 1962–1991

—■— DIVIDENDS   —⊖— EARNINGS

QUARTERLY OBSERVATIONS ARE IN JAN, APR, JUL & OCT

reflected in Figure 5-1, period "A." The yield investor seldom gets a chance to own a stock like Coca-Cola, but, as has been shown, RDY offers opportunities that are too exciting and valuable to pass up!

PepsiCo. PepsiCo was impacted by some of the same industry influences as was Coca-Cola. It hit a price bottom in 1982, not as a result of entering the movie business, but because of bottle inventory write-offs in the Philippines and a scandal in Brazil. There were also concerns about a slowdown in the growth of the snack food business, an important contributor to PepsiCo revenues, in addition to the soft drink industry's margin difficulties. But, at no time during the period of RDY attractiveness was the operating cash flow less than three times the dividend. Most investors were so focused on quarterly earnings growth that they forgot to consider value.

Like Coca-Cola, PepsiCo is now again a market favorite, with the aura of a growth stock reestablished. From an RDY of over

100% of the market's yield at the bottom of expectations in both 1980 and 1984 (see Figure 5-3), the stock price has risen more than fivefold, dividends are up 100%, and the RDY has dropped to under 50% of the market's yield.

Campbell Soup. Campbell Soup is another example of how RDY provides a mechanism for isolating investment portfolio decisions from the fads and despairs of the marketplace during the market's cycles. For example, after reaching an RDY above 120% for several years in the early 1970s (see Figure 5-4), Campbell Soup did almost twice as well as the market to January of 1975. At that time, the RDY reached 80%, or a 20% discount from the market's yield. By 1981, Campbell Soup had become unpopular again—so unpopular that the RDY reached over a 40% premium yield or an absolute yield of about 8%.

What had changed? Not very much. Earnings growth had slowed, but investor expectations for the future changed much more than the company's true prospects. Since the end of 1981,

FIGURE 5-3

PepsiCo, Relative Dividend Yield, 1962–1991

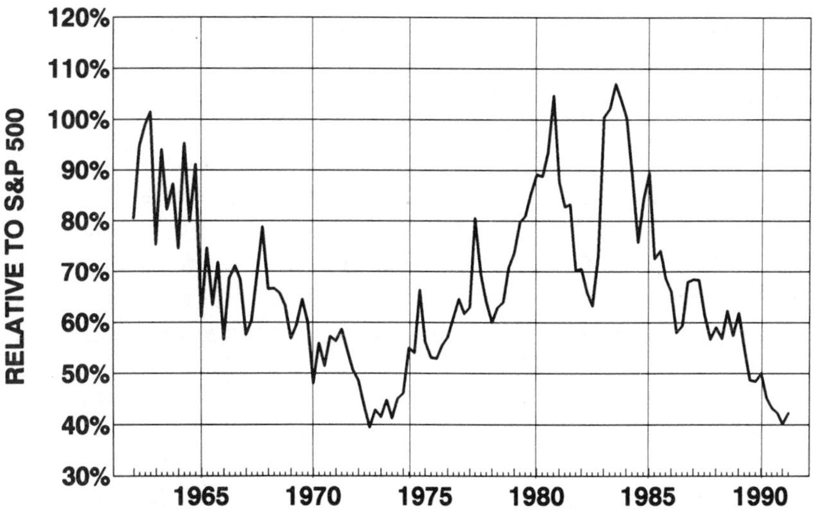

QUARTERLY OBSERVATIONS ARE IN JAN, APR, JUL & OCT

69

FIGURE 5-4

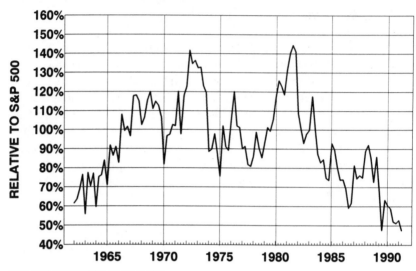

Campbell Soup, Relative Dividend Yield, 1962–1991

QUARTERLY OBSERVATIONS ARE IN JAN, APR, JUL & OCT

Campbell Soup has gone up almost four times more than the S&P 500 as a result of the general interest in the group as well as recurring merger rumors. At its current RDY levels, the stock is expensive. By the end of 1990, the RDY reached its lowest level in the nearly 30-year period covered by the data.

This is not to say that the stock cannot go up more. It is not, however, cheap. If earnings grow rapidly, or if there is an acquisition, or if the company borrows heavily to go private, the stock could continue to do well. When a stock is cheap in terms of RDY, the odds of a stock's providing positive surprises to investors are greatly increased. When a stock is expensive, *everything* has to go well in order to maintain its current price or to spur an advance.

Tobacco

Philip Morris. Any reasonably informed investor can make educated guesses. Consider the tobacco industry. Smoking has

70

been banned in public places, in offices, on planes—and who knows where next. Nonsmokers say that they are hurt by the smoke of others, and there are many, including members of Congress, who believe smoking should be banned altogether. How can anyone buy a tobacco company? Should you not let your subjective judgment come into play and override what the RDY discipline might be telling you?

But, if you think about the probabilities, in order to make an educated guess, what is the worst that is likely to happen? A total ban on cigarettes does not seem likely, at least not in the foreseeable future. Assuming the stock is then attractive according to RDY, should you buy it? You can look at the company's cash flow and long commitment to the dividend and say to yourself, "I still don't think there is enough of a likelihood that they'll cut the dividend or cut it so far that I won't still earn that extra 200—or even 150—basis points that make it worthwhile to hold the stock."

Concerns about the future provide opportunities for those investors following the RDY discipline. Philip Morris is a prime example, as its history of dividends and earnings shows (see Figure 5-5). While many investors waited for the tobacco industry's problems to sink the company, management made a number of acquisitions in the food industry. Though cigarettes still account for over 50% of earnings and cash flow, the company has shown its ability to use these earnings to fund further diversification. The emotionalism of the investment community is very clear in the RDY history of Philip Morris (see Figure 5-6).

This does not mean that the stock cannot move lower if further problems for the tobacco industry arise. It may well do so. But, if you still feel the dividend is safe, you just buy more of the stock whenever it is cheap enough. At these junctures, most people will be shouting, "Don't buy this stock! The company is going up in smoke!"

We have heard such warnings for the 16 years that we have used this discipline, and I know how few of the worst fears are realized. Sometimes the Cassandras are right, however. Chapter 7 will look at the pitfalls of the RDY discipline and how to prevent them. But the returns that the approach has generated over those 16 years prove that the ability to buck the emotionalism, defy the naysayers,

FIGURE 5-5

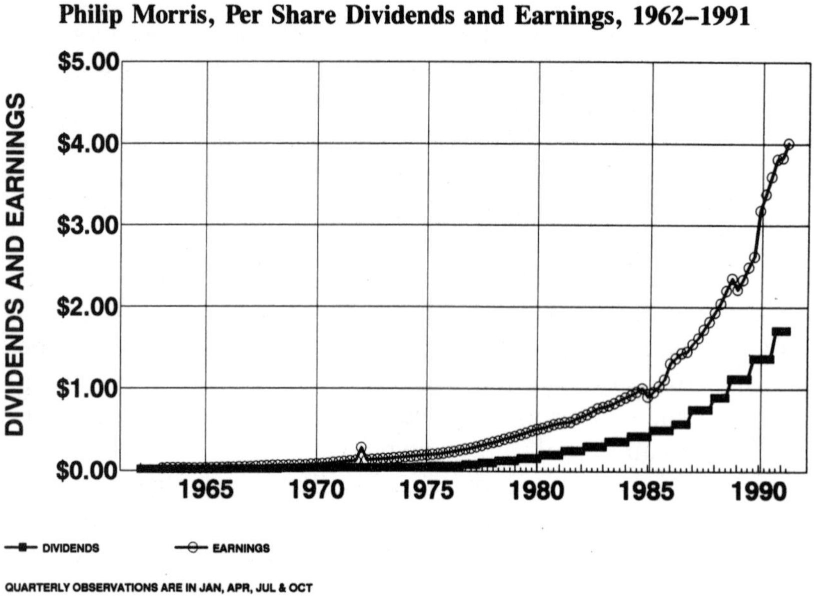

Philip Morris, Per Share Dividends and Earnings, 1962–1991
$5.00
$4.00
$3.00
$2.00
$1.00
$0.00
DIVIDENDS AND EARNINGS
1965
1970
1975
1980
1985
1990
DIVIDENDS
EARNINGS
QUARTERLY OBSERVATIONS ARE IN JAN, APR, JUL & OCT

FIGURE 5-6

Philip Morris, Relative Dividend Yield, 1962–1991
200%
150%
100%
50%
0%
RELATIVE TO S&P 500
1965
1970
1975
1980
1985
1990
QUARTERLY OBSERVATIONS ARE IN JAN, APR, JUL & OCT

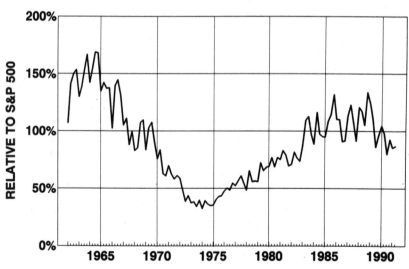

and ignore the negatives pays off handsomely. This is what contrary investing is meant to do. The approach allows you to ignore the pessimism and the noise and to just ask, what is the Relative Dividend Yield saying? If it is telling you to forget the rampant fear and to buy the stock, then you simply go ahead and buy it. Relative Dividend Yield hands you a tool—one that you know, through logic and history, works and that gives you the courage to defy prevailing opinion.

Retail Trade

Sears Roebuck. Nothing seemed to be going right for Sears Roebuck at the end of 1990. Management was castigated for lacking direction—or changing direction, from being a brand-name store to functioning as a discounter—and for providing poor merchandising in terms of group margins and earnings that kept going downhill. But, in looking at Figure 5-7, we see that we have lived through this scenario before with Sears.

From 1962 to 1977, investors did not demand a high yield from Sears; at that time, it was selling at a price where its yield was half the market's yield. But, by 1980, Sears went through a transition from a growth company to something less than a growth company. Inflation was hurting: Sears could not mark up the price of its goods to cover its high fixed costs without driving away customers, and there were some problems with its Allstate Insurance unit. In 1980, when Sears's yield was 180% of the market's yield (period "A"), no one liked the stock. Then, in the early 1980s, opinion reversed itself: The stock's price went up dramatically in the early bull market of 1982 and 1983, and the yield fell back below a market yield (period "B"). Then came another cycle, and people who loved Sears in 1983 detested it by 1990. Sears's stock was priced to pay a 6% yield, or about double that of the market (period "C").

This does not mean that Sears is not having very real problems today, when the yield is high. The key questions are, *Can* the company pay the dividend and is it *committed* to paying it? Despite the problems, earnings and cash flow look strong enough to sup-

FIGURE 5-7

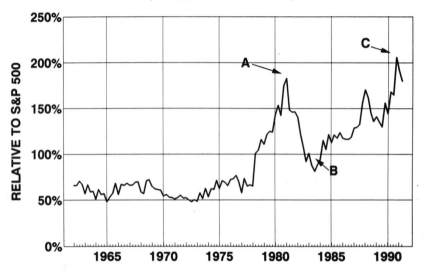

Sears Roebuck, Relative Dividend Yield, 1962–1991

QUARTERLY OBSERVATIONS ARE IN JAN, APR, JUL & OCT

port the payment (see Figure 5-8). The tool of RDY has proved to be reliable in the past. The company's earnings prospects will inevitably change, and the investor is getting well paid to wait!

Drugs

Eli Lilly.   The drug industry is usually out of bounds for income-disciplined investors because of its nearly invariable superior earnings prospects. Every once in a while, however, a problem causes enough concern about the future prospects of one or another of these stocks that they sell at an above-market yield.

Figure 5-9 indicates that Eli Lilly sold at an above-market yield several times in the early 1960s and the mid-1980s. Figure 5-10 highlights the period of 1978 through 1990 in greater detail. Eli Lilly reached a yield almost 10% above the market's yield at the end of 1984, when there were concerns about a lack of new drug

74

FIGURE 5-8

Sears Roebuck, Per Share Dividends and Earnings, 1962–1991

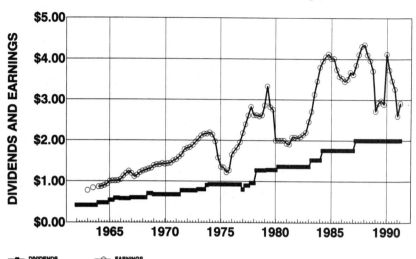

—■— DIVIDENDS   —○— EARNINGS

QUARTERLY OBSERVATIONS ARE IN JAN, APR, JUL & OCT

FIGURE 5-9

Eli Lilly, Relative Dividend Yield, 1962–1991

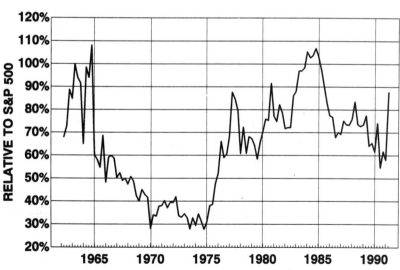

QUARTERLY OBSERVATIONS ARE IN JAN, APR, JUL & OCT

FIGURE 5-10

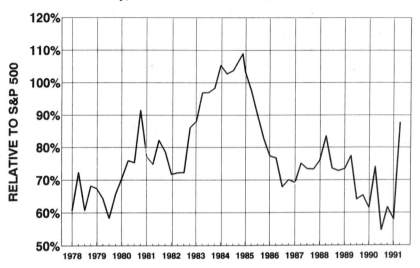

Eli Lilly, Relative Dividend Yield, 1978–1991

QUARTERLY OBSERVATIONS ARE IN JAN, APR, JUL & OCT

products from the company and worries about the growth rate of its agricultural chemicals division. Eli Lilly's absolute yield was consistently above 4% and even reached 5%. It was a rare buying opportunity.

Since then, Eli Lilly has achieved a price advance, to the end of 1990, about three times the market's rise. The company, with a strong new-product flow, is now one of the market's favorites. All of the concerns reflected in the high RDY of the mid-1980s are now gone. Few investors even remember that there was a time when Eli Lilly sold above a market yield and that it was very unpopular.

Bristol-Myers. Bristol-Myers has sold above the market's yield only during the last few years (see Figure 5-11). There were concerns about the dilution of the company's future earnings and the problems of integration when it acquired Squibb. The restructuring of the business caused a one-shot charge and reported earnings per share to drop below the dividend rate. The feeling that the

FIGURE 5-11

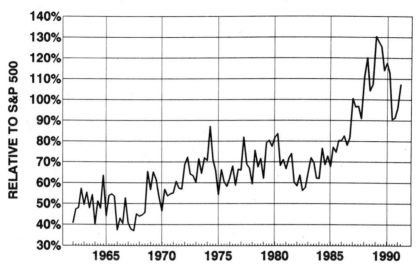

Bristol-Myers, Relative Dividend Yield, 1962–1991

QUARTERLY OBSERVATIONS ARE IN JAN, APR, JUL & OCT

merger would cause considerable earnings-per-share dilution was reflected in the historically high RDY.

The concerns have not become a reality, and the company even raised the dividend rate in 1990 as an indication of its confidence in the future. Bristol-Myers advanced from $41 to $67, or more than a 60% increase from the end of March of 1988, when the RDY was 120% of the market's yield, to the end of 1990. This compared with the 27% price change for the S&P 500 over the same time period, from $259 to $330.

Pfizer.   Because of concerns about the safety and product liability of a heart-valve product, Pfizer's RDY reached 115% in 1989, as indicated in Figure 5-12.

Figure 5-13 shows, however, that like many fallen-angel growth stocks, Pfizer maintained earnings levels that were well above the dividend rate. The RDY clearly helped isolate the emotionalism of the investment community.

77

FIGURE 5-12

Pfizer, Relative Dividend Yield, 1962–1991

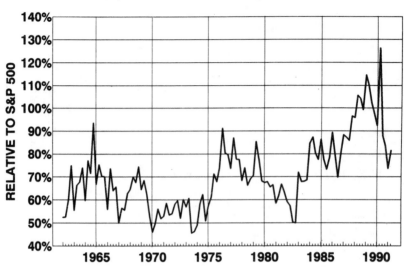

QUARTERLY OBSERVATIONS ARE IN JAN, APR, JUL & OCT

FIGURE 5-13

Pfizer, Per Share Dividends and Earnings, 1962–1991

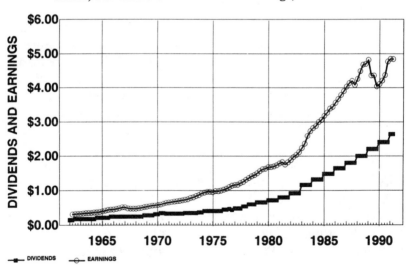

QUARTERLY OBSERVATIONS ARE IN JAN, APR, JUL & OCT

Since mid-1990, the RDY has again fallen below the market's level as the price has risen from $57 at the end of April to $81 at year-end 1990. During the same period, the S&P 500 declined slightly in price. In addition to the price increase, investors collected an above-market yield on the Pfizer dividend stream.

INDUSTRIAL STOCKS

Office Equipment

International Business Machines.   When you think of growth stocks, International Business Machines (IBM) has to be one of the first names that comes to mind. Since the 1930s, when punch card equipment preceded today's electronic machines, this company has been a consistent ideal of outstanding management, growth, and honesty in the conduct of its business affairs. Because of its success, the company (and the computer industry) has experienced the maturation that eventually comes to all companies. Computers have become so pervasive in the conduct of everyday life that they are now this generation's capital goods.

The RDY history on IBM, as indicated in Figure 5-14, shows the stages through which this company has gone. IBM was selling at a rapid-growth-stock yield of less than 50% of the market's yield until 1974. As the company matured and its growth slowed from above 30% toward the 20% range, IBM and the rest of the computer industry entered a transition period of slower growth. Since the expectations had been so high for the company, the reality of slower growth was a great disappointment to most analysts and investors, and the yield began to rise.

It was not until the period of 1980 to 1982, however, that the dividend yield rose above a market yield, as Figure 5-15 indicates. The absolute yield moved above 6%, but the RDY was at a 20% premium above the S&P 500 (period "A"). IBM returned to investor favor from 1982 to 1985, and the RDY fell well below the market's yield. Then, with continued slower growth than the company budgeted for in the late 1980s, earnings came under pressure.

79

FIGURE 5-14

IBM, Relative Dividend Yield, 1962–1991

QUARTERLY OBSERVATIONS ARE IN JAN, APR, JUL & OCT

FIGURE 5-15

IBM, Relative Dividend Yield, 1978–1991

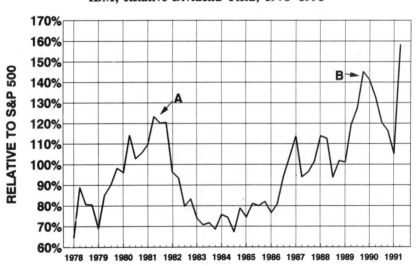

QUARTERLY OBSERVATIONS ARE IN JAN, APR, JUL & OCT

A series of year-end write-offs and early retirement programs resulted in another period of disappointing earnings. With little earnings growth, the stock's dividend yield rose until it offered more than a 40% premium above the S&P 500 yield of 3.5% in December of 1989 (period "B"). Based on RDY, IBM was even more attractive relative to the market at the end of 1989, when the yield was 5%, than it was in 1982, when the stock's yield was above 6%.

Figure 5-16 graphs IBM's per share dividends and earnings since 1962. The earnings provided strong coverage for the dividend payments being made throughout the period until the first quarter 1991 massive write-off.

Now that the management of IBM has taken a more conservative approach to its forecasts of future growth for the industry and the company, earnings are expected to rise. As of mid-1991, the RDY has risen far above the market's yield level.

The company might again become a great 15%-a-year growth company and no longer provide an above-average yield. If this

FIGURE 5-16

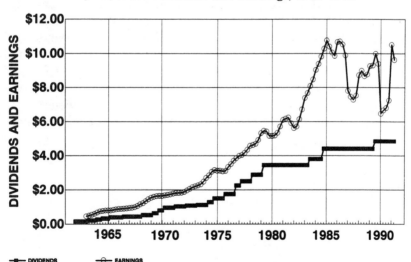

IBM, Per Share Dividends and Earnings, 1962–1991

—■— DIVIDENDS   —⊖— EARNINGS

QUARTERLY OBSERVATIONS ARE IN JAN, APR, JUL & OCT

happens, investors who buy the stock in late 1991 will reap significant profits from capital appreciation. At the same time, these investors will have benefited from the high-dividend-yield income stream.

Xerox. When the commercial development of xerography started in the early 1960s, Xerox became the ideal emerging growth stock for a generation of investors. Looking for "the next Xerox" was the consuming passion of many people for years. As happens to most other companies and industries, however, Xerox attracted new competition, and the saturation of the market resulted in the maturing of the industry.

When the company announced the acquisition of Crum and Forster (an insurance brokerage company), Wall Street and the investment community felt the company would never be a growth company again. Few investors were still interested in looking at the values in Xerox, whose cash flows could easily support the dividend for a number of years. When the company entered the insurance industry, that entire industry was attractively valued. The market did not care; it sold heavily out of frustration and contempt.

Those who did look at value and the various sources of earnings and cash flow have come to a very different investment conclusion. After having sold at a yield of less than 20% of the market's yield during its growth phase, Xerox was providing a yield that reached almost 2.5 times the market's yield by late 1990 (see Figure 5-17). If the dividend is safe, the value indicated by RDY is worth heeding. The company has recently been discussing a renewed focus on the image/copier business. They are also planning on leaving the financial services sector.

FINANCE

Banks

Citicorp. Citicorp had been a growth stock through most of the 1960s, 1970s, and early 1980s, as reflected in its low RDY (see

FIGURE 5-17

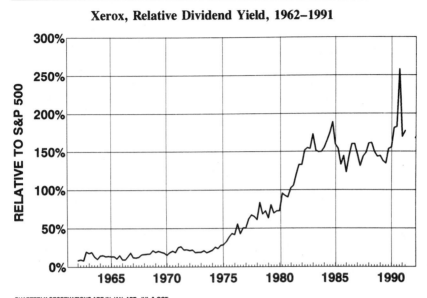

Xerox, Relative Dividend Yield, 1962–1991

QUARTERLY OBSERVATIONS ARE IN JAN, APR, JUL & OCT

Figure 5-18). With the declining inflation rate after the peak of 1983, borrowers were not able to pay back loans with cheaper dollars. Then came a rash of problems—first the LDC (lesser developed countries) loans, followed by the petroleum loans, the "rust belt" loans, and, finally, the leveraged buy-out and real estate loans. After years of steadily increasing dividends, Citicorp declared in late 1990 that they would cut the quarterly rate in early 1991.

As Figure 5-18 indicates, the RDY reached levels reflecting an anticipation of a cut in the dividend. Despite increasing their dividend for *each* of the previous 19 years, Citicorp management decided to cut their dividend in late 1990. By the time the cut was announced, there was very little impact on the stock's price since it had already declined 67% the previous year from $34 to a low of under $11. The historic pattern of dividends and earnings (see Figure 5-19) underlined the recent earnings problems and volatility. Since these problems had become fully appreciated by mid-1990, by the time the cut was announced, the value of the

FIGURE 5-18

Citicorp, Relative Dividend Yield, 1962–1991

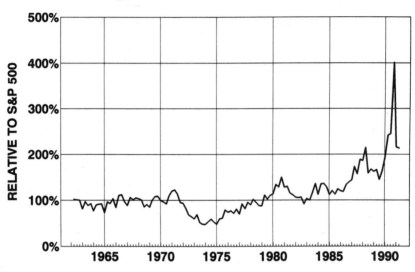

QUARTERLY OBSERVATIONS ARE IN JAN, APR, JUL & OCT

FIGURE 5-19

Citicorp, Per Share Dividends and Earnings, 1962–1991

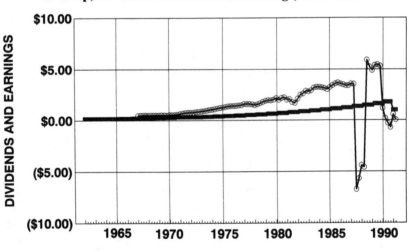

QUARTERLY OBSERVATIONS ARE IN JAN, APR, JUL & OCT

shares went up to $13 per share. As is true of most aspects of economic life, when the returns look too good to be true, they usually are. (*Note: On October 15, 1991, Citicorp suspended the dividend.*)

Personal Loans

Household International. Household International has been one of the leading companies in the personal, small-loan business for many years. Its RDY shows that it was considered a maturing, slow-growing company from 1974 to the early 1980s (see Figure 5-20). The investment community then became impressed by the company's growth rate spurred by its entry into the home equity loan business. The RDY declined sharply, from 200% to 100%, in 1988. With the concerns about declining real estate values escalating during 1989 and 1990, however, Household's RDY rose sharply. During the real estate panic in the period of August to October of 1990, the RDY reached 260% with an

FIGURE 5-20

Household International, Relative Dividend Yield, 1962–1991

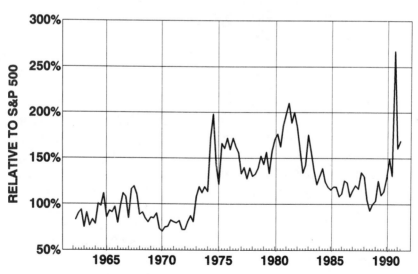

QUARTERLY OBSERVATIONS ARE IN JAN, APR, JUL & OCT

85

absolute yield of over 10%. Unlike Citicorp and other major banks, Household's earnings provided a large cushion above the dividend. From the fall of 1990, Household's stock rose over 100% in less than six months from a low under $20 to well above $40 per share, and the RDY declined to 150%.

UTILITIES

Telephone Companies

American Telephone & Telegraph.   The split-up of American Telephone & Telegraph (AT&T) in 1983 did not do much to change the company's historical RDY pattern. AT&T's RDY graph is not much different from that of companies like GTE, whose operations did not have to be distributed among regional operating companies. By the fall of 1989, AT&T's yield had dropped below the market's yield, as indicated in Figure 5-21. The absolute yield was below 3%. Since that time, AT&T's stock price has been a below-market performer, and the RDY has risen back above 100%. However, if the past is any indication of the future— and many times it provides a good guess—AT&T is still not cheap at the recent RDY levels.

Electric Companies

Texas Utilities.   For years, the utility industry has been considered a traditional-income stock group. This was not always the case, however. The RDY pattern of Texas Utilities (see Figure 5-22) or of any of the other electrics shows that in the early 1960s, most of the companies were achieving superior results during a period of general earnings stagnation. They were classified then as growth stocks. By late 1967, however, Texas Utilities had reached a market yield, and it has sold at an RDY above 100% of the market since 1971.

The escalation of inflation in the 1970s generally buoyed indus-

FIGURE 5-21

AT&T (Old and New), Relative Dividend Yield, 1962–1991

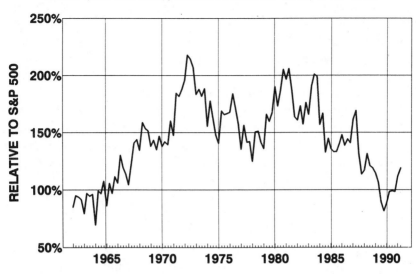

QUARTERLY OBSERVATIONS ARE IN JAN, APR, JUL & OCT

FIGURE 5-22

Texas Utilities, Relative Dividend Yield, 1962–1991

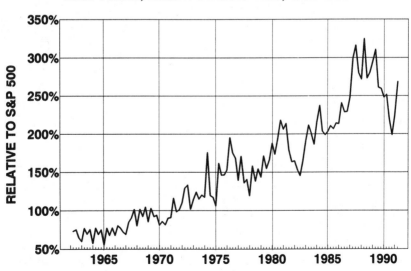

QUARTERLY OBSERVATIONS ARE IN JAN, APR, JUL & OCT

trial earnings growth, but utilities earnings lagged. In the 1980s, it was common for electric utilities to sell at twice the market's yield, with the exception of the period from 1981 to 1983, when concerns about economic recession led investors to utility stocks as a haven, causing RDYs to drop.

With the late 1980s came the panic about most companies with nuclear facilities. The RDY of Texas Utilities reached over 300% in 1988, or three times the market's yield. The absolute yield for the company exceeded 10% (see Figure 5-23). Reported earnings did decline in this period, but they never dropped below the dividend level, as indicated in Figure 5-24.

The company's stock, along with the majority of utilities, has failed to keep up with the general market's capital appreciation since the early 1960s. But a part of the total return on any invest-ment is the income stream. Dividend payments have been an important and rising portion of the return coming from utility investments, and, therefore, their total return has been quite good.

FIGURE 5-23

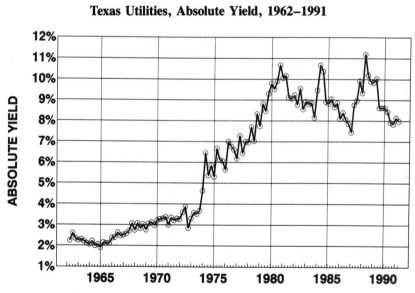

Texas Utilities, Absolute Yield, 1962–1991

QUARTERLY OBSERVATIONS ARE IN JAN, APR, JUL & OCT

FIGURE 5-24

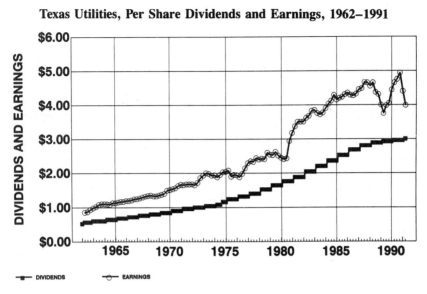

Texas Utilities, Per Share Dividends and Earnings, 1962–1991

QUARTERLY OBSERVATIONS ARE IN JAN, APR, JUL & OCT

CYCLICALS

Energy Stocks

Exxon. The RDY graph for Exxon (see Figure 5-25) illustrates once more how RDY provides information about basic under- and overvaluation periods for the purchase and sale of stock. Figure 5-26 offers the pattern of per share dividends and earnings.

During the 1980s, the oil industry experienced a period of major consolidation—Chevron's acquisition of Gulf Oil was the prime example. Exxon spent this period getting out of its ill-conceived diversification efforts of the 1970s. Nevertheless, until the Valdez oil spill, investors using RDY to determine periods attractive for purchase and sale of most stocks in the oil industry would have found few major differences among them.

FIGURE 5-25

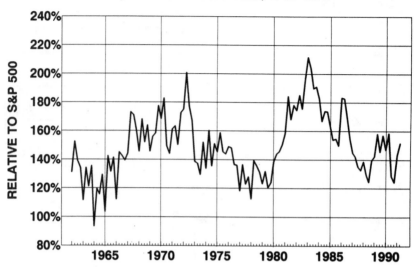

Exxon, Relative Dividend Yield, 1962–1991

QUARTERLY OBSERVATIONS ARE IN JAN, APR, JUL & OCT

FIGURE 5-26

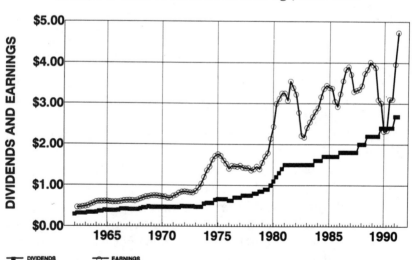

Exxon, Per Share Dividends and Earnings, 1962–1991

DIVIDENDS   EARNINGS

QUARTERLY OBSERVATIONS ARE IN JAN, APR, JUL & OCT

Texaco. The RDY graph for Texaco (see Figure 5-27) provides valuable investment information until 1987. The company had acquired Getty Oil but then had been sued by Pennzoil, which claimed it had a previous agreement to buy Getty. To protect the financial position of the company, Texaco filed for bankruptcy and omitted the dividend. Without a dividend, investors cannot use RDY, and the stock would have had to have been sold unless the investor was willing to make some assumption about the final resolution of the suit. From the time of the dividend omission to its reinstatement, Texaco's stock reached a low share price of under $30 and then quickly rebounded to a price in the high $30's. After its agreement with Pennzoil, the dividend of $3.00 per share was reinstated, and the use of RDY in evaluating Texaco's attractiveness was again possible.

As can be seen from Figure 5-27, the RDY method indicated that Texaco, with a dividend yield more than 50% higher than the market's yield, was attractive once again. Texaco's recent history of paying extras raises another important point. The dividends used

FIGURE 5-27

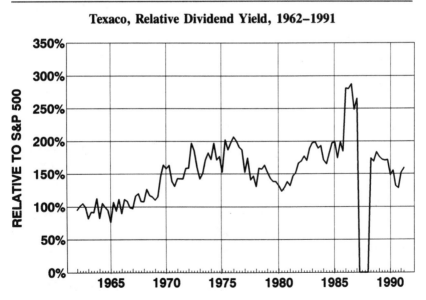

Texaco, Relative Dividend Yield, 1962–1991

QUARTERLY OBSERVATIONS ARE IN JAN, APR, JUL & OCT

in this calculation did not include the extras paid as part of Texaco's restructuring in 1989.

Only the annual rate of regular dividend payments is used as the base rate for the RDY computation. Extra payments made by many companies as part of restructuring activities or as a defense against raiders, as often occurred in the 1980s, do not catch the swings in investor emotions that are the core of using RDY successfully as a valuation technique. Managements do not establish extra payments based on the criteria so important to the determination of an appropriate dividend level—normal sustainable earnings power—which also reduces their validity to the RDY process. As more companies adopt extra dividends tied by formula to their earnings, the separation of the base rate from the total dividend will become more important.

Forest Products

Weyerhaeuser. As mentioned, the cyclicals are a major sector of interest for RDY investors. The reported earnings of cyclicals are subject to the operating leverage typical of many maturing companies. When revenues fail to reach budgeted levels, earnings fall sharply. For many commodity-based industries, like forest products, sales volumes and product prices move up and down together, causing the revenue volatility to be particularly severe and unpredictable. Focusing only on most-recent quarterly earnings would not indicate the ability of a company like Weyerhaeuser to continue to pay its dividend. Its resource base and confidence of its directors and management in the future prospects of the company are expressed in the dividend, not in the reported earnings (see Figure 5-28).

Figure 5-29 shows the emotional swings that investors in Weyerhaeuser have gone through over the past 30 years—from disinterest ("A") to enthusiasm over a perception that Weyerhaeuser had become a perpetual growth company ("B") to recent disinterest once again ("C"). The emotional swings provide the favorable periods of accumulation and disinvestment.

FIGURE 5-28

Weyerhaeuser, Per Share Dividends and Earnings, 1962–1991

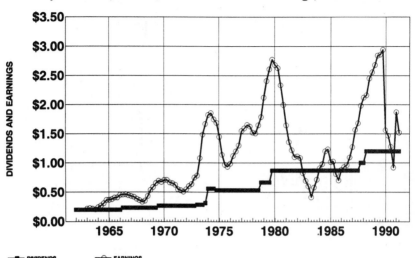

QUARTERLY OBSERVATIONS ARE IN JAN, APR, JUL & OCT

FIGURE 5-29

Weyerhaeuser, Relative Dividend Yield, 1962–1991

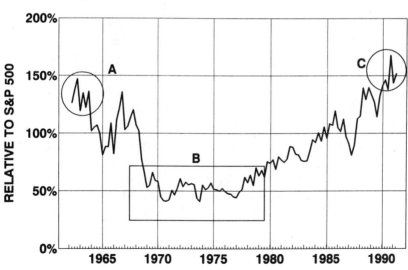

QUARTERLY OBSERVATIONS ARE IN JAN, APR, JUL & OCT

FIGURE 5-30

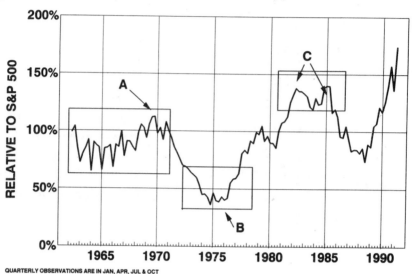

Dow Chemical, Relative Dividend Yield, 1962–1991

QUARTERLY OBSERVATIONS ARE IN JAN, APR, JUL & OCT

Chemicals

Dow Chemical.   Investor perceptions and emotions concerning Dow Chemical, a growth-cyclical, are easily picked up using RDY. Over many years, the company has grown and increased its market share of the world's chemical industry. As it has matured, Dow has not been able to grow as rapidly as it did in its formative years. Figure 5-30 indicates this progression, as reflected in the trend toward a higher RDY; compare period "A" with period "C." Over time, the RDY level at which Dow is attractive may be going up, but in period "C" it reached a level that was likely to mark it as a "cheap" stock and a worthwhile value. It is also probable that the beginning of a sell range will move commensurably higher than the range established during period "B."

6

PITFALLS AND PREVENTATIVE MEASURES

MAINTAINING A SAFE DIVIDEND LEVEL

One of the major problems that can arise in using RDY stems from the dividend level. While the obvious concern is a dividend cut, dividend increases that may bring stocks into attractive ranges must also be watched. Since RDY is used as a valuation technique for generating capital appreciation as well as for the higher income stream it generates, the level of the dividend payment is a critical factor in the approach.

It is not that cuts are always followed by a decline in price or that a dividend increase is followed by a rise. Most of the time, changes in the dividend rate have been anticipated by the market. Nevertheless, a cut in the dividend might make the stock unattractive, depending on how much the stock price has already dropped or appreciates after the cut. Sometimes, the likelihood of a cut is obvious to even the most casual investor. When a stock's yield, based on the most recent annual rate, reaches some preposterous level that is far outside anything in the company's history, the market is almost surely predicting a cut. A yield of five to six times the market for a stock whose yield would normally be high at twice the market's yield clearly signals a cut. Many times, management has already announced an intention to cut at the next meeting of its board of directors, but the data base has not been adjusted to reflect this coming event.

Dividend cutting seems to run in cycles that are usually related to the external economic environment. At first, any cuts come as a surprise, and the stocks whose boards have taken action go down after the cuts. Then, a stage is reached where cuts are expected among troubled companies, and prices change little after the cuts. Finally, a period is reached when there is such a great level of concern about dividends that the actual cuts are often less than the actions anticipated by analysts and investors, and the stock rises after the cuts have been announced because the uncertainty about the size of the cuts has been lifted.

Just because there is a cut does not mean terrible consequences for shareholders. The use of RDY as a valuation technique directs people into stocks that are so cheap that very often a cut does not affect the share price very much.

In addition to earnings that do not cover dividends for an extended period of time, other factors that cause managements and boards of directors to lower the annual dividend rate include increases in debt and debt-servicing obligations and the installation of new management. A new chief executive may decide to "clear the deck" and start from a low base to guarantee that he or she will look successful thereafter; write-offs and dividend cuts are common measures. Though analysis of such factors to forecast dividend action can improve investment results using RDY, such research is not necessary to achieve superior returns.

An example will clarify how a dividend problem that could not have been easily anticipated can arise. In the case of BankAmerica in the early 1980s (and other banks in the late 1980s), the fact that dividends were not covered by earnings for several quarters at least placed investors on notice of the possibility of a negative dividend action. Eventually, the Board of Directors of BankAmerica took the drastic action of cutting the dividend and then eliminating it altogether.

Starting in 1980, BankAmerica sold at an above-market yield and had an increase in RDY from the level of four years earlier as indicated in the following table:

12/31	RDY	RDY Change from Four Years Earlier	Following Four-Year Total Return
1980	102%	39% points	−20%
1981	130%	55% points	−1%
1982	155%	79% points	−8%
1983	167%	80% points	−56%

Was there any warning? Yes, but not very much. The dividend was covered by reported earnings until 1983. The dividend cut did prove to be a good forecast of future earnings problems, but not much information was provided just by reported earnings levels at the time.

Such dire results for an individual holding obviously pull down a portfolio's total returns achieved. Specific-issue problems can be dealt with either on a diversification basis or by securities analysis. Owning a smaller proportion of stocks with higher levels of potential problems will reduce the impact of the problems and make the portfolio less volatile. Chapter 3 demonstrated empirically that RDY alone can generate superior returns. Fundamental research is not necessary. Our experience at Spare, Tengler, Kaplan & Bischel is that research and experience can further enhance total return while lowering risk levels. Following is a broad discussion of the fundamental research we have employed in managing RDY portfolios.

EXAMINING COMPANY FUNDAMENTALS

When a stock has fallen in price until its historical RDY has entered the zone of attractiveness, the next step at my firm is to examine the fundamentals of the company. This is the primary reason we have analysts—not to generate ideas but to check the soundness of the companies we are considering for investment. The companies have problems—we know that from the stock price—but how bad are these problems? Most specifically, we want to know whether the dividend is safe, because if the dividend is slashed substantially or omitted, the stock can no longer be judged by using the RDY discipline.

Relative Dividend Yield is a tool to identify value, but it is not a computer-driven, black-box system. Other investors may have decided that the companies in which we are interested are anything but interesting to them, and the stocks' prices may have fallen to reflect this disfavor. We want to have the knowledge that will allow us to establish a different view of a company, and thereby have the faith that its troubles are exaggerated or temporary, before we buy it. We want to be as sure as we can that the troubles are not threatening and weed out the one company whose problems are critical.

If you buy the best-known companies like IBM, Citicorp, Sears Roebuck, General Motors, and Eastman Kodak, you should have considerable confidence that the extra portion of analysis you undertake is not critical to an assumption that the companies are still powers to be reckoned with. And, if you own a dozen such well-known stocks, the prolonged troubles of just one are not going to threaten your returns. Thus, even the individual investor, who lacks the resources to do extensive research, should do well following the RDY discipline.

MAKING EDUCATED GUESSES WITH PROBABILITY ANALYSIS

The safety of the dividend rests, obviously, on earnings and cash flow. Companies invest their own considerable analytical power in making the dividend decision and make it with a longer-term perspective than Wall Street research applies. Boards and managements make judgments about what normal, stable, sustainable earnings power is when they set the dividend.

The investor must look at past earnings streams to see whether they have been sufficient to cover the dividend. A dividend that has not been covered for 8 consecutive quarters of trailing 12-month earnings is a warning signal.

Examining cash flow is just another way to get at normal earnings power. Almost no one who is a successful value investor relies solely on reported earnings. Often, they do not supply what you need to know; usually, cash flow does.

The investor also needs to look at a company's debt level. A company with little debt that runs into earnings problems has the ability to borrow, in effect, to maintain the dividend. Balance sheet analysis is important to us. We certainly prefer tight financial controls and conservative accounting practices; we want to know that earnings are not a reflection of accounting gimmicks that will later backfire. We compare the companies to their peers on both a balance sheet and a liquidity basis.

Financial ratios aside, we like our companies to be market or product leaders who dominate their industries. They should have an above-average level of normal profitability compared with other companies in the industry. Another factor we look for is management depth, so that the departure of a few key managers would not be devastating.

All of this kind of information, which is necessary for making educated guesses, is quite readily available from annual reports, analysts, and management. In reality, you do not usually get every positive factor you might want in order to go ahead with the establishment of a position. For example, you may know that some companies' balance sheets are just not as good as you would prefer, but since these companies happen to be market leaders in a stable industry, the financial risk really is not too great. If their businesses do not present much risk, then they can afford to take on more debt. On the other hand, if their industry does entail high business risk, then you want to be sure that they have not compounded it by taking on too much debt.

USING A STRAIGHTFORWARD
ANALYTICAL PROCESS

The RDY investors start with one advantage: They do not need to look at hundreds of companies. Since all stocks that do not have above-market yields are eliminated from consideration, only large companies are left.

What any RDY investor can try to do, then, is to analyze the dividend-paying culture of a company's directors. What are their criteria for judging the dividend? How are they going to deal with the stress of earnings that are not covering the dividend? Are they willing to borrow to continue payment?

Wall Street analysts are not much help in deciding the attractiveness of an RDY stock. While they are very knowledgeable in details and facts, with their elaborate earnings models, they often lose perspective on what the company is worth, or when it is cheap or expensive.

Wall Street analysts are also too short-term oriented; they seem able to look only at earnings for the past 12 months. In general, they are too pessimistic when earnings decline and are too optimistic in good years. In short, they get swept up in the emotions of the market. By the time RDY investors are attracted to a stock, Wall Street analysts have usually lost interest. Thus, it is vital to the RDY approach to challenge the consensus.

100

Free cash flow—net income plus depreciation and deferred taxes and minus capital expenditures and dividends—is very important. Dividends are paid out of cash flow, not earnings. An electric utility that builds a plant may be reporting earnings, but there is no cash flow. There are many measures of cash flow, but we use a simple one: We ask whether or not the company will be able to cover its dividend payments with the flows of cash through the business.

Cash flow is different among different industries. One industry may have very high depreciation charges and another, low charges. We have to consider the capital intensity of a particular industry. Some industries can continue for a long period of time without heavy expenditures. In other industries, capital expenses are cyclical. Electric utilities, for example, go through major building phases; then, when a plant is completed, their capital expenditure needs trail off for several years. We also pay close attention to maintenance capital expenditure levels. A company may be able to forego some expenditures, but maintenance costs are not among them.

In assessing cash flow (and thus the dividend), we look at the history of companies, taking into account the industries they are in and trying to ascertain anything that might change past patterns. How has management reacted in other difficult periods? If it is a cyclical industry, how did it respond during the last downturn? Is it a fallen-angel growth stock? If so, it may be difficult to gauge because very often these stocks have not had to face difficult times before.

It is especially important to note that the majority of the companies have *never* cut their dividend. This fact makes our analysis straightforward: If a company has historically earned 14% on equity and is currently earning only 7% on equity—barely covering its dividend—people get very nervous. But, if we see the industry recovering—for example, the paper products industry, where we know that as capacity is consumed, the capacity utilization rate goes up and return on equity is going to move back closer to its historical norm of 14%—we know that earnings will rise and that the dividend is probably safe.

101

In talking to management, evaluating whatever public statements have been made, and making use of our knowledge about the company's behavior in similar periods in the past, we arrive at an assessment of the corporate culture. These companies do have dividend cultures. There may have been an earlier period when the stock was yielding twice the market's yield and the dividend was never cut. The market thinks there is risk, and there is risk—but it may not be substantial risk. The probabilities are that the dividend is safe.

Of course, since management has a vested interest in painting a rosy picture, we can't take management's word wholesale. Many times, management will release a statement that the dividend is safe and then later reverse its decision. And, if top management has changed, the fact that the dividend was always paid in the past may not be a sound indicator. New management has no commitment to the record of the past and may want to bring a whole new image to the company.

Georgia Pacific is an example of a negative surprise resulting from changed personnel. Georgia Pacific is a cyclical stock that goes through periods of undervaluation detectable through examination of dividend yield. The early 1980s were such a period, and we talked to the chief financial officer of the company, prodding him to tell us under what circumstances he would cut the dividend. He replied, very emphatically, "There's no way we'll cut the dividend. We are committed to it." If he had stayed at Georgia Pacific, he probably would have prevailed. He was fired, however, and the board decided that the policy he had voiced so vociferously in the investment community also had to go.

This kind of event is one of the few perils the RDY investor faces, and almost every year one stock proves to be a disappointment. Consequently, the approach must be used in a diversified portfolio. You cannot let one disappointment impact total portfolio returns too negatively.

In summary, expectation of a dividend cut is not necessarily a signal to stay away from a stock. What counts is how big the cut will be. As mentioned, there are times when a stock has gone up after the dividend has been cut because the stock was beaten down to the point where all the uncertainty was removed. There are also times

102

when a larger-than-anticipated cut has not been a disaster simply because the stock was already so cheap. We do have a rule, however: When the dividend is dropped altogether, get out of the stock because the RDY valuation technique can no longer be used.

FOCUSING ON QUALITY COMPANIES

A quality orientation is another important characteristic of RDY-based investment portfolios. Our insistence upon quality companies is not merely a reflection of conservatism. High-quality corporations enjoy many advantages that give the investor confidence so that when problems do arise, there is a more-than-reasonable chance that the companies will be able to overcome them. These advantages, and the criteria that define desirability, were spelled out by Philip Fisher in his 1957 book *Common Stocks and Uncommon Profits*. Although Fisher's interest was growth and emerging-growth companies, we have adopted my old teacher's advice, which has proved to be invaluable to the success of the RDY approach over the course of more than 16 years. The advantages that a quality company possesses are discussed next.

- *Industry leadership and profitability:* High market share and volume relative to the competition are important in any industry. Business leadership gives a company the ability to spread costs over a larger number of units. This in turn results in lower unit costs and the ability to control the competitive environment. Smaller competitors cannot afford some of the expenditures that help perpetuate the company's leadership position. High-market-share companies typically enjoy higher gross margins. The gross profits can be used for research and marketing and for manufacturing improvements. An investor has to examine each market segment or product line in determining market share. There are some very large companies with many divisions, none of which has a strong market-share position.

  High-gross-margin companies tend to have the lowest cost of manufacturing, the highest-quality products, the best sales and service organizations, and the ability to turn out new products that command higher margins. An industry leader tends to perpetuate itself if the company is well managed and if there are no changes in technology or other disruptions in the industry.

The market leaders may not be the firms with the highest aftertax margins. Well-managed companies spend for the future in a way that prevents customers, suppliers, and competitors from discovering just how inherently profitable they are. If the profitability is too obvious, suppliers raise prices, customers want discounts, and competitors enter the marketplace. High-net-profit companies may not have been spending enough on the future. Net margins that are too high reflect a monopoly power that seldom can be maintained.

- *Conservative financials:* Both conservative accounting and strong balance sheets provide flexibility and a cushion to weather adversity. It is not unusual for the best companies to have earnings disappointments earlier than their weaker competitors when the industry experiences a slowdown in demand for its products. Because of their financial strength, these companies continue to do the long-term spending that their weaker competitors cannot afford. The weaker competitors may cut back on expenses and try to maintain earnings because of more precarious banking and financial market relationships.

  The financially strongest and most conservative companies have the flexibility to take a longer view. They can be more aggressive with their products and services. Conservative accounting practices require the maximum expensing of costs and the minimum amount of capitalization of expenses on the balance sheet. Enterprises that are conservatively accounted for can spend more in the future because they are not burdened by the absorption of old costs into the current earnings stream.

- *Information systems:* Knowing what is going on within a company becomes ever more important in retaining industry leadership. Control of the flow of materials, money, information, and product is an increasingly vital competitive weapon. From purchasing through manufacture and sales to shipment, such information is critical. Fewer days of inventory on hand and fewer days of receivables outstanding reduce financial pressures. In addition to the financial benefits from better information and controls, there are customer-service benefits that allow higher prices that in turn result in higher margins.

The best companies tend to deal with the best companies. Being a desirable customer to its suppliers puts a company in a strong bargaining position when necessary. The best customers get materials during periods of product shortages, and they are not pressured during periods of excess supply. Suppliers may offer bargains to companies with the highest credit ratings and most secure financing, which may reduce costs and increase margins for years into the future.

- *Leadership in quality control:* Doing something right the first time is cheaper than having to redo it. Defective and returned merchandise is not only expensive to handle but also causes customer dissatisfaction and a reduction in repeat orders. There are financial benefits in being the best. Higher margins, for example, can be reinvested to maintain the repetition of this positive cycle so that advantages are reinforced.

- *Cost of capital:* Market leaders borrow at cheaper rates and sell securities with less dilution to existing shareholders. Higher price/earnings multiples and lower interest costs are yet another set of cost and cost-per-unit factors that make it very difficult for less financially sound firms to compete.

Section II

APPLICATION OF RDY
TO PORTFOLIOS

7

**RDY-BASED PORTFOLIO
CHARACTERISTICS,
CONSTRUCTION,
AND MAINTENANCE**

PRIMARY CHARACTERISTICS OF
RDY STOCK PORTFOLIOS

The RDY approach has consistently performed well over the years because of the constant maintenance of the portfolio characteristics discussed next.

High Yield

The most obvious characteristic that RDY stocks share is high yield. As noted, no stock is admitted to a portfolio if its dividend yield is below the market's yield. The average yield for RDY portfolios has been at least 50% higher than the market's yield. The RDY is a tool to identify undervalued stocks but the dividend yield also contributes significantly to total return. Over time, half of RDY's total return comes from dividend income, which is not as out-of-line with general experience as might be expected. Various studies of long-term returns on stocks indicate that the dividend yield accounts for almost half of the total return. An average yield of about 4.5% plus capital appreciation of about 6% has provided a total return of about 10.5% for equities since the mid-1920s.

Low Risk

Another extremely important characteristic of RDY portfolios is their low risk level. During the many years of managing RDY portfolios, their beta (a measure of portfolio return volatility versus the S&P 500 of 1.0) has been about 0.75. This, of course, is not only surprisingly lower than that of the market but also far lower than that of most professionally managed portfolios with similar objectives.

Why is this so? It is not because of the use of cash. The objective of this approach is to be fully invested; the average cash position is thus about 5% or less. As is true of any value discipline, there are times when the values simply are not available in the market, and higher cash positions may result. The use of investment reserves,

110

however, has not had a major impact on either the returns or the risk levels of RDY portfolios.

There is no market timing element. Rather, RDY invests in a class of securities and seeks to realize the returns available from this class of securities over time. It is the RDY discipline itself that leads to low volatility. It is a characteristic of the stocks in the portfolios. Specific stocks purchased under the RDY strategy have been undergoing a difficult period in the marketplace; in most cases, they have underperformed the market for some time. They may have once been stocks with high betas, but by the time high yields indicate their attractiveness to the RDY discipline, they tend to be beaten down, washed out, and of little interest to investors. No one wants to buy them, and since they have already been sold by those who hate them, there they sit. They become relatively inactive, and this neglect is likely to continue for some time. Therefore, when RDY signals them as buys, they are beginning a period when they will evidence less volatility than they have recently experienced and less than that of the market.

At the time of purchase, their beta is usually below that of the market, and during the period when they are held, their volatility is considerably less than that of the market. Another interesting result of the RDY strategy is that the beta of a total portfolio, containing stocks purchased at various stages of their cycles, has resulted in a beta less than the weighted average of the constituent securities. This is unusual and is a result of how the portfolio is constructed. This topic of portfolio construction will be discussed in detail later in this chapter.

Management of the RDY strategy—the construction of portfolios in light of this discipline—results in the purchase of what consequently prove to be low-volatility stocks. The biggest risk remaining in the stocks, in most instances, is that their price will continue to do nothing for some time. Since a portion of total return for the RDY investor comes from the dividend stream, the investor collects income while waiting and can afford to be patient. This income stream is consistent and, indeed, grows over time. It can keep up with the rate of inflation; the purchasing power of the stock's income stream can be maintained over the long run.

111

Diversification

Diversification also helps to keep the beta low. The RDY approach provides a wide range of attractive stocks. Low variability of returns and a low beta are the results.

Typically, managers who are in the very top decile in short-term performance rankings have highly concentrated portfolios in the winning industry group for the quarter. If, for example, both electric utilities and energy stocks are attractive according to the RDY valuation technique, the RDY investor would own both industry groups. They would likely be weighted differently in the portfolio according to their level of attractiveness as indicated by RDY, but both groups would be owned nonetheless. Typical highly concentrated portfolio managers would bet on either the utilities or the energy stocks. If they are right in a given quarter, they are in the top decile. If, however, they are wrong, they are likely to end up in the bottom decile. Such managers take a great deal of specific risk from their belief in sector rotation. This type of concentration is not appropriate for the RDY-disciplined user. By owning both utility and energy groups, if cheap, the RDY investor gives up the opportunity to be the big winner on a short-term basis but also avoids the possibility of being the worst loser. Over longer time periods, the power of being a "median" performer on a quarterly basis compounds to top-decile performance over three- to ten-year periods, with less-than-market volatility.

The fact that the RDY investor buys large, mature companies also lowers the beta of the portfolio. The portfolio is full of familiar, well-known companies. Since holdings are large-capitalization companies, and because RDY dictates that positions are accumulated over time and sold over time, liquidity is not a problem.

Although attractive RDY investments are well-known stock names at the time of purchase, most are not well thought of by the investment community. This is why their yields are high relative to their past histories as well as relative to the market as a whole. But this is what a value investor does: By definition, he or she can find bargains only among stocks that are out of favor.

112

Long Holding Periods/Low Turnover

Another characteristic of RDY portfolios is low turnover. The typical stock holding period is three to five years. Turnover, therefore, runs 25% to 30% annually, or about half the rate of most managers. Since reduced trading obviously saves transaction costs, more money is left to compound over time, which contributes to the RDY discipline's superior returns. For taxable accounts, low turnover has the added benefit of lowering the capital gains tax burden.

Consistency

The consistency of all of these portfolio characteristics is an important factor in assessing the ongoing success of the RDY approach. The discipline must be maintained. Consistent characteristics result in reliable returns. High yield, quality stocks, low volatility, and long holding periods have to be adhered to as is true of any discipline. These characteristics are not something imposed by portfolio managers; they are imposed by the discipline itself and are essential to its success. Reviewing characteristics quarterly is a very effective way to determine whether everything is "in control" during a given market cycle and to keep an investor "honest." Perhaps institutional-fund sponsors tend to focus too heavily on short-term performance when judging their managers. What they really should be looking at is the consistency of the characteristics of their managers' portfolios over a reasonable time period to make sure that each plan's needs will continue to be met.

ASSESSMENT OF RDY STOCK PORTFOLIO RESULTS

The RDY approach is not theoretical or untested. My colleagues and I developed the use of this approach in portfolios managed in the early 1970s. We have been practicing and refining the process for nearly 20 years. Chapter 3 showed what even a mechanical application can achieve, and the data in Appendix B summarize the empirical work on yield and relative yield change conducted by Jack Brush at Columbine Capital. Assets managed under the RDY discipline have realized returns that have approximated these results, exceeding market returns with less-than-market risk. Since most investment styles have done no better than the market, particularly during the last 10 years, the discipline has obviously outperformed most others on an absolute *and* risk-adjusted basis.

Time horizons are an important factor in reviewing success. In the short term, the results of any strategy can be discouraging. The investor must be patient. For a single quarter, even for a year or more, expensive stocks can get more expensive and continue to do well, as they did in 1990. Sometimes, expensive stocks get ridiculously expensive. Sometimes, cheap stocks stay cheap for a very long period.

Over time, however, value is recognized and gets expressed in rates of return. Investors cannot be certain exactly where their results will fall in the short term, but the characteristics of their portfolios should achieve competitive returns with below-market risk over the long haul.

To reiterate, results do have to be measured and evaluated over more than a few months or quarters. High-yield value strategies need to have enough time for dividend reinvestment, the compounding effect, to work. Patience is imperative for the inherent value in the stocks to be recognized. Many investors find it more exciting to focus on the latest takeover stock in their portfolio or dwell on the price moves of insignificant percentage holdings in the best-performing industry group for the quarter. The RDY approach is hardly "exciting," but it has provided impressive results.

In a highly speculative environment, the RDY investor cannot be expected to do as well as the market as a whole or as other managers. He or she takes less risk. Value investors, who shun the stocks that are being driven to ever-higher prices by investor euphoria, are seldom at the top of the heap in raging bull markets. But the RDY investor will have a diversified portfolio, and while some of the stocks will do little, others—those that may have been bought several years ago and have passed through their confidence restoring stage—will behave well. Absolute performance will be

114

respectable, but relative to those investors taking more risk in frothy markets, the RDY investor will lag.

WHY THE RDY DISCIPLINE WORKS

One of the main reasons why the RDY approach achieves superior returns over time is simply that portfolios are continually earning 200 to 300 basis points above the market yield. More importantly, the use of RDY as a valuation technique helps to select cheap stocks to be purchased and expensive stocks to be sold.

The RDY investor is able to match or exceed market price change in all but the most speculative market periods. This style of investment also experiences portfolio declines that are less than the averages in periods of extended market downturns.

The RDY discipline forces the investor to buy stocks when they are undervalued and sell them when they are moving into over-valuation. Market emotionalism pushes stocks to prices where they just should not be. It is the old "fear and greed" syndrome (see Figure 7-1). Emotionalism, overcoming all the solid information that we have about companies, keeps the market from being efficient. Using RDY takes advantage of this inefficiency.

Fear is almost always present when a stock is "cheap" because it is always cheap for a reason—and the reason typically is that the company has not been doing well. The earnings growth rate has fallen. An enormous increase in dividends is usually not what makes dividend yields so high relative to their past; it is company problems. When RDY stocks are bought, the companies usually continue to do poorly for a time. They are bought so cheaply that they usually do not fall much farther. Because these stocks are inherently cheap, the odds are in the investor's favor.

Nevertheless, it takes courage to buy at these points. You take a risk when you buy a stock that is hated or neglected. There are either real or perceived negatives. An investor is not going to make money, however, if he or she is not willing to take risk—especially what others think is risk. What the value investor expects, in reality, is to get paid for uncertainty. The investor in venture

FIGURE 7-1

The Cycle of Fear and Greed (STK&B, Inc.)

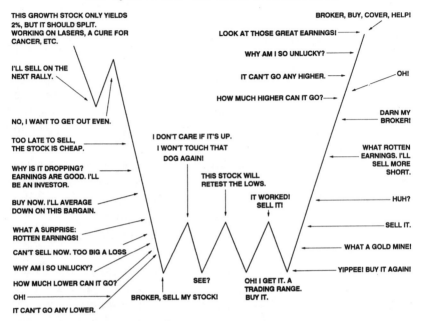

capital or emerging-growth companies hopes to get paid for the uncertainty that these fledgling companies face. The investor in mature companies, by the same token, expects to be paid for uncertainties that arise about them: Can they continue to dominate a market? Keep up with new technology? Compete with newer and faster growing companies? Can they, in a word, "survive" and pay the dividend?

The extremes of the investment spectrum, viewed from the perspective of uncertainty, tend to be close together. Emerging and maturing companies have many uncertainties about their futures. This is similar to what is often said about politics: Radicals of the right and left are closer to one another than they are to the people in the center.

Investors in large, stable growth companies, on the other hand, are buying their stocks with a high degree of confidence that all is well for the future. When everybody knows, loves, and understands the story—like that of the Procter & Gambles and Mercks of the world—they perceive only very low levels of uncertainty. Thus, these investors are willing to pay a premium price for these stocks.

Value investors, however, expect to get paid for uncertainty. When historical RDYs are high, you usually have the greatest uncertainty. To deal with this uncertainty, you must have confidence in your investment tools and realize when you have been through similar situations before—that IBM in the late 1980s may be like Du Pont 15 years ago and General Motors 25 years ago. They were never again the same companies that they had been, but this does not mean that you could not have made money in them. IBM as a $65 billion company in 1991 cannot be the same as it was in 1965, but you have to realize that money can be made in IBM now in spite of all the uncertainty about the viability of mainframes and all the questions raised when earnings growth slowed or fell for a few years.

The RDY investor gets paid, then, for dealing with other people's uncertainty and is rewarded for their misconceptions. If you have a discipline, if you know something about the company, and if your time horizon is long enough, you are the beneficiary of their uncertainty. You earn a risk premium, and you earn this premium rate of return because you know more about how to look at the company's value. The average investor focuses on the problems without regard for value. The RDY approach provides a different way of looking at value.

The real challenge, in managing a portfolio, is to be sure that you are taking *enough* risk. If you buy 50 middling stocks, then you are going to end up with a middling rate of return, and even with this return, on a risk/reward basis, you might not do as well as if you had indexed. You must make sure that you are assuming sufficient risk—challenging accepted beliefs—and that you are then controlling the risk at the portfolio level. You are taking the risk of buying companies that you believe you understand, but that you suspect most of the world either does not or is just not paying attention to.

The compelling characteristic of the RDY approach is that it provides a way to be challenged into a different opinion. The only real fear that you have to deal with is the dividend safety: If you believe the dividend will be paid (at some level), you can go ahead and take a position. Although the safety of the dividend is a judgment call—no one is going to be able to tell you, "It is an absolute certainty that this dividend will be maintained for the next three to five years"—analysis can be done to put probabilities well in your favor, as will be shown later. In any case, a well-diversified portfolio will not suffer critically if a few calls are wrong.

FOREIGN STOCK APPLICATION

An important question is often asked about the RDY discipline. It arises because investors have become increasingly international in their portfolios, and they naturally ask whether the RDY discipline is applicable to foreign stocks. Thus far, the answer has to be, no. The United States is one of the few countries in the world whose equity market lends itself to the RDY approach to investing. We have major companies with long dividend-paying histories. Investors are able to use dividends in helping to identify under- and overvaluations. Japan does not have companies with this kind of history; the United Kingdom, Canada, and the Netherlands all have a few. But, in terms of the world's total supply of stocks, the United States has a near monopoly on the kind of stocks needed for the RDY discipline. Capitalism has simply been operative here longer. If you look at Europe, for example, many big-name companies were privately held for many years, then nationalized, then privatized again. Many have been torn apart and put together as a result of wars. We have had far greater stability in the United States. In time, the picture will undoubtedly change.

WHY RDY IS NOT BETTER KNOWN

At present, a relatively small amount of assets appears to be managed according to the RDY approach. If the discipline is so straightforward and makes so much sense and has proved that it can provide better-than-market returns with such a low level of risk, why is it not more popular?

One reason has just been discussed and should not be underrated: It takes courage to be contrary, and this kind of courage is rare. When you buy stocks when they are at their cheapest, they are truly pariahs. The RDY traders continually have to listen to other traders who say, "Are you crazy? Everybody hates these stocks." Wall Street analysts argue, "Why do you want to have 'dead money' stocks in your portfolios?"

It is also not easy to sit and suffer through some down quarters in a stock because you happen to be early. If managers have to beat the market every quarter to please clients, this discipline would never be the one for them. Many investors are short-term oriented. The RDY approach takes time to work. In an era when consultants, pension-fund administrators, and money managers are avidly comparing quarterly, even monthly, results, RDY's quarter-to-quarter results are not usually going to command much attention.

The RDY approach is conservative, which means that it will usually underperform in soaring bull markets, when growth stocks command ever higher multiples. It has, however, outperformed the market significantly over time.

Not only is RDY conservative, it is also even a little dull. You own mostly the stocks that no one cares about, and there is little action in them for a long time. Not much excites the imagination because you are rarely going to own a stock that doubles in six months. The stocks that others find exciting, that investment professionals talk about among themselves, and that the press writes up are rarely being purchased in RDY portfolios. Only those investors interested in making a higher return while taking less risk are excited about this approach. But, after all, what could be more exciting?

PORTFOLIO CONSTRUCTION: MORE THAN JUST A BUNCH OF STOCKS

Most institutional investors fail to take advantage of the opportunity to act less like securities analysts and more like the portfolio managers they are. Wall Street securities analysts are forced, by the nature of their clients' requests, to discuss stocks on an issue-by-issue basis. They are also asked to give opinions for very short periods of time. Suppose an analyst were asked about a stock's likely performance and responded, "I don't know when it will go up. But it's cheap, and you will make a lot of money over the next five years if you buy it now." The analyst would probably be fired.

You never know whether a cheap stock will get cheaper. As with all stocks used in the RDY approach, the investor has the opportunity to use time and diversification as allies in the investment process. All shares, even of a single company, need not be purchased at once. Shares of all companies do not have to be purchased at the same time. Diversification is the proper response to the "unknowns" typical of cheap stocks. Most institutional investment managers are too concerned about the binary decision to "own" or "not own." Not enough attention is paid to the effect of *weighting* various issues. After all, the impact on a portfolio's performance is greater if you own 3% of an issue rather than 1%, but the usual concern is over owning 1% versus 0% of the same issue. The management of an RDY portfolio allows the gradual accumulation of positions and different weightings for each stock depending on the quality of the company. The idea is to buy at a lower average price and sell at a high enough average price to beat the market and other investment managers at each level of risk.

It is not unusual for stocks to drop in price after the RDY investor has started to purchase them. Indeed, the hope is that they do. If they began to move up immediately, the investor would not be able to average in and accumulate as meaningful a position. Since the investor can never know just exactly how far a stock will fall—it is cheap when it is bought, but it can get cheaper—an intended position is not taken all at once; purchases are averaged in *over time*. If the stock does fall after the initial transactions, the investor knows that more can be bought to round out his or her position at a lower price. For example, the stock of the so-called CBA Corporation is cheap at point "A" on Figure 7-2 (the RDY is above the beginning buy point of 115%), but it is cheaper at point "B."

120

FIGURE 7-2

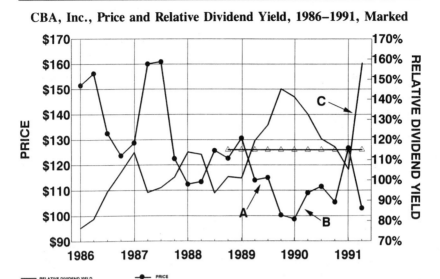

CBA, Inc., Price and Relative Dividend Yield, 1986–1991, Marked

Institutional investors should not promise what they cannot deliver. While everyone would like to purchase his or her entire position in every stock at the lowest relative price, it is simply not feasible. Since the RDY investor is interested in the average price paid for the entire stock position, the cost of any one purchase becomes almost irrelevant.

The RDY investors are sometimes offered the opinion that their initial buys show poor judgment, even when other portfolio managers agree that the stock is cheap at the time of purchase. When these managers are asked whether they own the stock or are going to buy it soon, they answer, no. When asked why not, they respond, "Well, I can buy it at the same price, or cheaper, later. Why tie up money?" In other words, they see the opportunity, but they do not take advantage of it.

Many investors want to be buyers just before a stock is about to take off, for example, perhaps at point "C" on Figure 7-2. But, since they have no idea when this will be—no one does—they end up never owning the stock or sometimes buying it at the peak. If you try to be "brilliant" in every buy or sell transaction you make, you will find the decisions so impossible that you will either never make a move or make roller coaster calls—remember the fear and greed chart of Figure 7-1?

In constructing RDY portfolios, there is the opportunity to diversify by industries, sectors, companies—and time. The investor needs to have time to buy and sell stocks. Some stocks in a portfolio are in the accumulation stage, while others are reaching a sell point.

PORTFOLIO DIVERSIFICATION

Time diversification complements industry and sector diversification. Usually, even the best analysis cannot supply satisfactory answers to the risks involved in industries and companies; the specific stock risks, therefore, can only be managed by diversification. Risk cannot be avoided by the equity investor. It must be managed and dealt with *intelligently*.

Investors who use the RDY strategy will end up with highly diversified portfolios. If the portfolios were assembled purely on an absolute-yield basis, there would be little diversification since many of the highest-yielding stocks have similar characteristics and are influenced by similar external events. When RDY is utilized to identify value stocks, the investor eliminates expensive stocks and buys cheap stocks, and cheap stocks are scattered over many industries—not just those with the highest yields. You can find them in cyclicals, in consumer nondurables, and in almost any and every industry. Nor are you ever going to find that every cyclical stock is undervalued or every consumer nondurable stock is undervalued. The use of RDY highlights cheap stocks across a broad spectrum of economic sectors and industry groups.

Because RDY investors are not interested in sector rotation based on a forecast of the economy or just on their feelings about which industry groups to own does not mean that an RDY portfolio does not change. It does change, but the changes happen slowly and are driven from the bottom up by the RDY discipline. If two stocks or two industries are equally attractive on a long-term basis, the RDY investor will own both. The inherent value of the stocks will direct the investor into and out of various industries.

The usual time period for most holdings is three to five years. During this time, the RDY investor may go from a zero holding in a stock or sector to a very large position compared with the S&P 500 and then back to a zero position.

There are many groups where high relative yields are available, but they move in opposite directions most of the time. Two such groups in the period of 1985 to 1989 were the oils and the electric utilities. Although both groups were cheap at the start of the period and did well for investors over the entire period, they did not do well concurrently each and every quarter. Because of this low covariance, the resulting portfolio volatility was less but did not limit the overall performance.

Groups are up one quarter, down the next. Sector rotators who try to catch the incoming winners quarter after quarter take on an impossible challenge. There is no record of any investor's consistently being able to pick which industry is going to be favored in any upcoming quarter. The RDY investor says, "I can't predict trends. If there are attractive securities, I will buy them." How much of each stock is owned will be a function of its relative attractiveness and certainty about the dividend payment. By diversifying, the likelihood of RDY's outperforming the market enough to be at the top of the performance derby in any given quarter is very low. The long-term returns for buying cheap stocks and selling expensive stocks are clear. The goal of the RDY portfolio manager is to achieve a good return over time while maintaining a volatility lower than that of the market.

Lower-than-market risk (as measured by volatility of return) is achieved due to several factors:

1. Cheap stocks do not have as far to drop as expensive ones do.

2. Diversification and low covariance among groups provide less portfolio volatility than individual stock volatility alone would indicate.

3. The high-yield income stream from above-market-yield portfolios provides a low volatility source of total return.

Diversification and low-covariance among sectors and issues are direct results of the RDY discipline.

Any investment professional who has dealt with the public knows that much of what has to be done is educational. The individual investor must be reminded not to panic in market drops, not to get swept up into enthusiasms, to diversify assets so that there is some protection under different economic environments, and to avoid doing things that are unwise. Individual investors should not feel that they are, therefore, egregiously naive and foolish. Such a view of themselves is unwarranted and, if held by others, is undeserved.

Professional money managers, who should do far better than individual investors, usually do not. Although they are trained to do investment work and they spend most of their time doing it, they are too often worried about their clients' looking over their shoulders. Many thus perform poorly despite their intelligence, degrees, data sources, and computer power. Individual investors have more independence. When the market tanked in 1973–1974, 1982, and 1987, many institutional money managers were terrified to move, fearing their clients' wrath. It was the individual investor who said, "This is cheap" and lifted the market from its bottom by buying stocks one by one. The main fault of individual investors is that they tend to sell too soon.

The demands on professional investors are not very different when they are investing for institutional and for individual clients. When you invest for a pension fund, after all, it is really individuals with whom you are dealing—whether professional staff, members of the finance committee or a committee of the board, the chief financial officer, or the chief executive officer. They think as individuals, and you still have to explain to them that they cannot get everything they want. In an up market, they want to keep up with the best, and in a down market, they want to earn absolute rates of return. Everybody wants—expects—to be in the first quartile in bull markets and to achieve a minimum 5% return in bear markets.

The right response to these desires is not market timing or some other form of magic, but the development of a proper perspective. Do not judge month to month or quarter to quarter or even year to year, but look at market-cycle rates of return. Look peak to peak or trough to trough, *not peak to trough*. Whether an individual or a pension plan sponsor, the investor must come to appreciate the vital element of *time*. You need time to reach your goals. Time is one of the most important elements in the investment management process, and it is usually not understood or valued enough.

Instead, people look for short-term results. They envy more aggressive investors with spectacular recent returns. Some investors do have terrific returns, even over a ten-year period, but almost invariably, after ten years or so, they are not able to sustain the same results. Their assets under management grow to a size where flexibility and liquidity suffer, and their psychology may change. Someone who has succeeded so long in the market may not be motivated to work quite as diligently as when he or she started a career. Results may still be good, but they may no longer be spectacular. Like the market itself, norms tend to reassert themselves.

The RDY investor takes a slower, but surer route. The RDY approach does not rely on the genius of a "stockpicker." It minimizes volatility, and it is a relatively simple discipline that can be applied with the same consistent results forever.

SAMPLE PORTFOLIO

Table 7-1 is a sample portfolio that might be used either by the individual investor or as a portion of a larger institutional account. The names listed are the largest 25 companies ranked by market capitalization out of the S&P 500 with both yields (as of June 30, 1991) above that of the market and a positive change in RDY from four years earlier (June 30, 1987). These 25 stocks account for over 17% of the entire S&P 500 capitalization. The average yield is over 40% above that of the market, at a 4.7% average yield compared with the S&P 500 yield of 3.3%. The RDY investor has a head start of 1.4% points above the market over the next 12-month period.

If the investor wanted an even higher current return, there are 20 out of the 25 largest capitalization stocks with a yield of 4% and over. These stocks have an average yield of 5.5% and account for over 14% of the S&P 500 weight. The fewer the number of stocks

TABLE 7-1

Sample Portfolio

Company	June of 1991		Yield	RDY	Four-Year RDY Change
	Price	Dividend			
S&P 500	$371.16	$12.07	3.3%	100%	0%
American Express	$22.50	$0.92	4.1%	126%	51%
Amoco	$50.63	$2.20	4.3%	134%	7%
Atlantic Richfield	$114.75	$5.50	4.8%	147%	6%
Borden	$34.88	$1.14	3.3%	101%	29%
Chevron	$70.38	$3.30	4.7%	144%	14%
Consolidated Edison	$24.63	$1.86	7.6%	232%	10%
Dow Chemical	$53.13	$2.60	4.9%	150%	65%
Dun & Bradstreet	$47.38	$2.16	4.6%	140%	60%
Du Pont (E.I.) de Nemours	$45.88	$1.68	3.7%	113%	23%
Eastman Kodak	$38.75	$2.00	5.2%	159%	60%
Exxon	$58.13	$2.68	4.6%	142%	12%
Ford	$36.00	$1.60	4.4%	137%	35%
IBM	$97.13	$4.84	5.0%	153%	62%
Kmart	$45.25	$1.76	3.9%	120%	27%
Minnesota Mining & Mfg.	$93.63	$3.12	3.3%	102%	14%
Mobil	$64.25	$3.20	5.0%	153%	8%
Morgan (J.P.)	$52.13	$1.98	3.8%	117%	21%
Nynex	$71.38	$4.56	6.4%	196%	14%
Penney (J.C.)	$53.00	$2.64	5.0%	153%	58%
Phillips Petroleum	$25.50	$1.12	4.4%	135%	14%
Sears Roebuck	$37.88	$2.00	5.3%	162%	30%
United Technologies	$44.50	$1.80	4.0%	124%	34%
Westinghouse	$27.88	$1.40	5.0%	154%	64%
Weyerhaeuser	$26.75	$1.20	4.5%	138%	51%
Xerox	$54.00	$3.00	5.6%	171%	40%
Average			**4.7%**		**32%**

and the lower the amount of diversification, the greater the volatility. With a higher absolute yield minimum, the diversification is reduced even more. For example, the only auto stock, both of the utilities, and all six of the petroleum stocks had yields of 4% or more.

It is interesting to note, with the change made in the composition of the Dow-Jones Industrial Average (DJIA) in early May of 1991, that 11 of these 25 stocks are also included in the DJIA. The RDY charts for all of the common stocks of these companies are included in Appendix C. If past results hold in the future, a portfolio of these securities when held over a four-year period should provide a total return above the S&P 500 when the dividends are included in the calculation.

RDY AND MARKET TIMING

Can RDY Help with Market Timing?

The answer to this question is that RDY does not attempt to time the market. It tries to focus on a diversified array of individual stocks. If RDY investors can find enough good ideas within the framework of a diversified industry and economic-sector structure, they will be fully invested. To the degree that they cannot find enough good names, they allow their investment reserves to build up.

Like most equity managers, we have clients who instruct us to stay fully invested because they take care of asset allocation. The truth is that any cash has hurt rate of return, not just since 1982, but for 15 years, because stocks have returned more than cash. One thing cash does do, however, is provide flexibility. Having reserves does make it easier to move from an expensive stock to cash to a cheap stock than it does to run a horse race between two stocks, selling one and buying the other. Cash also further reduces the variability of the portfolio return.

Our focus is on cheap stocks, and when we do not find enough of them, we end up building reserves, at least to some degree. An investor wants to go with the odds. If, by looking at individual issues, we find values, we buy them; if not, we do not press the matter. However, there were enough attractive stocks, for example, to be fairly fully invested from the fall of 1981 until the spring of 1986. The major market index bottom was not reached until August of 1982, and the market did not peak until August of 1987, followed, of course, by the sharp decline in October of 1987.

Two factors work in favor of RDY investors who stay nearly fully invested through all market cycles. First, since they earn an above-average yield, they are paid to wait during market slumps. They pick up 200 to 300 basis points as a cushion.

Second, many of the stocks that the RDY investor owns near market tops are the kind of traditional-income stocks that tend to be defensive in nature. These stocks will often get cheaper in the tail end of a bull market and lose their cheapness after the early stage of the new bull market. Electric utilities are the obvious example. They stop going down when the rest of the market is still falling and often start to move up when the market as a whole is still in a decline.

Very often, in a declining period, the RDY investor's stocks have hit bottom already. Their superior relative performance starts to show up simply because they are not going down anymore or are going down at a much slower rate than the market as a whole. People do recognize the fact that there is little risk left in the stocks. They also do not argue that the stocks are cheap. But analysts do not recommend them because they are considered "dead money." The feeling is that the stocks can be bought at the same price later or maybe even bought at a cheaper price.

Can Timing Ever Work?

In theory, market timing should add significantly to the rate of return. In practice, however, there have been very few successful investors who have relied on market timing. A 1989 Sanford C. Bernstein study entitled "Stock Market Timing: It Still May Be Hazardous to Your Wealth" concluded that during the last ten years, "if you had been out of the stock market during the best five months (that's *five* months out of 120 or *110* days out of 2540!) during the decade, your return on stocks would have degraded to a return not much above the risk-free return produced by T-bills"— well below a fully invested strategy. With the market increasingly characterized by intense bursts of activity, timing is even more difficult. Trends change quickly. By the time a trend can be identified, it may have changed again. With the trend basically upward over time, maintaining reserves is a bet against the odds. In short, you have to be in it to win it!

You can kill your returns by trying to be too clever. If a stock is cheap and you are paid to be patient, why try to outguess yourself? A holding period in the three-to-five year range is normal for the stocks that fit into the RDY strategy. If the average return per stock is 50% to 100%, the resulting rate of portfolio return is very good. The capital appreciation plus the dividend stream generates a longer-term rate of return that is above the probable market return and above that of most other investors.

Just as it is difficult to time the overall market, it is even more difficult to time individual stocks. It would not be unusual to start to buy a stock, for example, at point "A" on Figure 7-3, as it enters an attractive price area, and see the stock decline and become even cheaper. In this case, the position can be increased. It is not unusual for there to be a long period when nothing much happens. But, eventually, as everybody begins to understand the value, the stock starts to climb, at point "B." Most people think that they should buy it at point "B," but no one has had a very good record of

FIGURE 7-3

CBA, Inc., Price and Relative Dividend Yield, 1986–1991, Marked

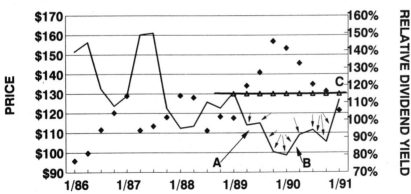

129

doing this with any regular success. We are interested only in our average purchase price, our average selling price, and the rate of return we earned. Most people in the investment industry do not disagree that the opportunity to go from "A" to "C" is desirable, but they try to be "smarter" by waiting to buy the entire position at "B" and end up outsmarting themselves.

A drop in price does not mean that a stock is cheap. Buying cheap stocks requires a benchmark or discipline to substantiate and reinforce the decisions. As Table 7-2 shows, the investor who buys true value can afford to hold for a long time and generate high returns from price appreciation alone if the eventual move is great enough.

Even having to wait a long time for the capital appreciation to materialize is acceptable if you are paid to wait by receiving a high enough current dividend yield. Assuming that the decade of the 1990s will see a total return from common stocks in the 10% to 12% range, even waiting for seven years and getting only a 50% price increase with a 7% yield stock will achieve better returns than the market, with less volatility. How can so many investment professionals agree that most of the stocks that are bought and owned with the RDY approach will advance 50% to 100% at some point during the following five years, and yet not own them? They try to be too clever and wait for everything to become clearer. Most of the time, these investors pay dearly for the added information. It is one thing to miss the first 30% move of a stock that may advance

TABLE 7-2

Impact of Holding Period on Rate of Return

Total Price Change	Annual Compounded Rate of Price Change Holding Period in Years			
	3	5	7	9
50%	13.6%	8.1%	5.8%	4.5%
75%	18.8%	11.3%	8.0%	6.2%
100%	23.4%	13.9%	10.0%	7.7%

200% or 300%, but 30% may be half of the eventual change in price for the usual RDY stock. Very good total returns can be achieved by combining dividend yield and capital appreciation for the patient investor.

If you look at the bull market of the 1980s, you see enormous swings in the popularity of groups from attractive, to unattractive, and to attractive again. This is why you have sector rotators; it makes a big difference to be in the right groups at the right time. But sector rotators have not been any more successful at this game than you can be at calling the market as a whole. The rotation is so rapid now that by the time you try to latch on to a trend, you are too late. To catch the momentum, on a technical basis, surely is too difficult.

As RDY investors, we have made major movements among sectors, not by trying to ride with identified momentum, but by buying groups when they are cheap, before they have started moving up. Cheapness, of course, is identified by our RDY evaluation technique. We are willing to wait until a sector is again in favor, which is quite different from trying to catch the flow.

Of course, looking at how the market is acting cannot be helped. Whether we are in a recession, recovery, or boom is something every reader of this book has a sense of. This does not mean that you can tell what GNP is going to be in the next quarter or forecast earnings for the next quarter. But the basics of where we are in a market cycle are what we know and care about. You may have an opinion about whether the market is cheap, at fair value, or very expensive. And you may, feeling strongly that the market is very expensive, want to unplug the RDY machine for a time and keep at least a part of your assets out of the market. Some may go to 20% cash and others to 80%. The actions taken are a function of the goals, objectives, and time horizon of the particular client and portfolio.

Portfolio construction is not just a matter of putting a group of cheap stocks together. Far more is required than looking at stocks one at a time. Most brokerage house securities analysts and newsletter writers, however, are forced into discussing stocks one at a time. They also consider very much shorter time periods than are appropriate for most investors.

Most analysts and portfolio managers try to time their purchases to the day when they can identify an earnings rebound or exceptional growth. They may admit that a stock is cheap, but they do not buy it because they are worried about the current quarter, the next quarter, or the next year. By the time anyone has been able to identify a definite uptrend, it is too late anyway. For example, IBM was attractive for a year and a half at the end of the last decade, and few investors were willing to buy it. Most waited until the stock was up 20% before they made a commitment—just before it declined 30% to under $100 with RDY once again over 170% and an almost 5% absolute yield. The RDY investors want to own companies whose managements are geared for the long run and are not trying to maximize profits just for the next quarter to satisfy Wall Street. Instead of getting in and out of a stock several times over a short period, they build a position patiently over time—and their patience pays off.

8

HAVING OTHERS INVEST FOR YOU AND INVESTING FOR OTHERS

THE CLIENT–INVESTMENT
ADVISOR RELATIONSHIP

The relationship between client and investment advisor is always a delicate balancing act. There needs to be an understanding of a client's goals and objectives, and a trust must be built between both parties.

The supervision of a team of investment managers is one of the most difficult tasks for any member of a pension-plan staff (or an individual investor) who hires an investment advisory firm. Hiring another party to manage assets has a number of variables attached to the process that make the selection and subsequent monitoring process very important.

Understanding Management Styles

The first challenge is to get to understand the manager's style. The client needs to fully understand the kind of financial market and economic environments that will allow the advisor to prosper and in which environments the advisor is likely to produce adverse results. No one style of management produces superior results in all time periods. No one style produces superior results regardless of the short-term climate for making investment management decisions. The *interaction* of the results of one manager with those of other managers must also be considered by the client when selecting managers to help achieve a plan's overall goals and objectives. Some investment styles complement and augment one another. Some styles may *sound* different, but the results are redundant and magnify the short-term volatility of the plan's returns.

The investment characteristics of most of the best investment advisors are very consistent. As just pointed out, however, some characteristics are more volatile than others. Price/earnings ratios can be high either because there is great confidence in the future growth prospects of a company or because earnings are depressed. Over time, a very close relationship develops between yield on a portfolio and the volatility of the rates of return. High yield and low risk go together.

134

Avoiding a Short Time Horizon

Each of the management firms has to be watched closely to ensure that it is not changing the discipline it was hired to execute. A well-thought-out plan, in which each manager is expected to play a specific role, will be destroyed if any one of the firms changes its approach. The most likely time for any management firm to change its discipline is after it has "failed" for a period of time. This is usually just before the approach it was hired to execute is about to "work" once again. The pressure placed by clients on managers to change comes largely from too short a time horizon. Internal conflicts as well as outside pressures can aggravate this short time horizon even when a firm's principals have an understanding of investment cycles. While few managers are hired without being told that they have three to five years, or a market cycle, to "perform," many clients still think their managers have failed after just one adverse year—or even one quarter. Perhaps the staff is being pressured by board members who may not have an understanding of market cycles. The pension consultant may be reinforcing a short-term focus.

Time is an essential element of any relationship. This is particularly true in the investment business. Most successful investment disciplines take time to unfold and provide the benefits to the employees and the company's plans that were anticipated or implicitly promised when the investment advisor was hired.

Matching Plan Size and Growth to Managers' Assets

One of the aspects of manager selection that has to be considered is the size of the plan and its growth in relationship to the size of the manager's assets. Some managers with certain styles can be very successful managing, say, $500 million, but when they reach $5 billion, they are doomed to failure. For example, a manager with assets of $500 million total in all its portfolios may own the same 50 stocks in each portfolio. If the advisor does not want to own more than 5% of the shares outstanding of any one company, he or she must own companies with a total market capitalization, on average, of $200 million. The same manager investing $5 billion is faced with the challenge of finding ten times the number of "great companies," or owning 50% of the best 50, or, on average, owning $1-billion-capitalization-size companies. Regardless of what course is taken—and it will usually involve some combination of these choices—the manager's style *will change*. Change may be for the better or for the worse, but there will be change.

Matching Plan Objectives to Managers' Styles

Every pension fund, profit-sharing plan, and endowment—or individual investor account—has its own objectives and should look for management styles to reflect these objectives. Each of these different pools of funds has a different time horizon determined by the risk of forced payouts. A pension fund with a young work force can own a greater proportion of assets with long time horizons, while a retired individual has a much shorter investment period. Insurance surplus pools for a life company have a different time horizon than a property/casualty company with policyholders located in hurricane country.

Matching Plan Requirements to Individual/ Organizational Life Cycles

Every plan and every individual has a "life cycle" that dictates investment time horizons and risk-taking ability. While this is more obvious for an individual, it is also true of a company, a union, an endowment fund, or a foundation. Every organization goes through a pattern of development, growth, maturation, and decline. Investment requirements should change to match this progression. Varied assets and different styles of investment management are called for during each of these periods.

Dealing with Cyclical Business Risk

An issue that is largely overlooked by many plan sponsors is that there may be an interaction between the pension plan and the cyclical nature of the sponsoring company's business. Each client should take a different approach to this issue. The character and nature of the company and its leadership may be such that management will want to take high risk in both the company and the benefit plans or take risk in neither. Some firms try to balance their business risks with those of the retirement plan's investment funds. Some are willing to take risks in the business and want lower volatility in their benefit-plan assets. No one answer can be applied to all circumstances. However, this issue requires more attention. The company in a cyclical business may want to reduce the volatility of its pension fund to avoid the need for significant contributions to the plan during a cyclical downtrend in earnings.

Communicating Effectively

Anyone working with outside managers has to communicate as many of the factors about his or her organization and its needs as is possible in order for each management firm to understand its place in the total picture and how that place is likely to change over time. In investments, as in war, Murphy lives: What can go wrong will go wrong—and at the worst possible time. The better informed the investment advisors are, the better they can anticipate and plan their own strategy while still following the disciplines for which they were hired. At the extreme, this would mean that an advisor would not accept an account or would resign from an account when the advisor's investment approach did not fit or no longer fit the client's needs.

THE INSTITUTIONAL VERSUS THE INDIVIDUAL ADVISOR

The institutional investment advisor has the same problems in selecting the appropriate assets, types of investment approaches, and time horizons as the clients have for themselves. The next chapter, which advises the individual on investing for himself or herself, should be read as an "investment consultant" to the "wealth-holder." The problems that face individuals managing their own assets will face you, the professional investor, as you try to provide for their needs. The questions that they must ask themselves, you too must ask of them if you are going to have a satisfied client.

9

INVESTING FOR YOURSELF

CONSERVATISM IN THE 1990s

Those at institutions responsible for assets today are usually well versed in modern portfolio theory and obviously more aware of and sensitive to the question of volatility and risk than individual investors might be. The average private investor is concerned with absolute rather than risk-adjusted returns. Nevertheless, although individual investors may not talk in terms of standard deviation of returns, the marked swings in the market are terribly disturbing to them. Many individual investors have been driven out of the market. This is particularly true of older people who do not have as many working and investing years ahead of them to recoup any losses. Demographics tell us that the population is aging; the percentage of the investment population that is older is therefore also growing. More attention is going to be paid to risk by individual investors than was paid in the past. This same longer life expectancy also means that there are more years for worrying about the ravages of inflation on the purchasing power of incomes and the value of accumulated wealth.

Another reason for conservatism in the 1990s is that there has been a huge increase in investor wealth. People are more interested in conserving their wealth now. From 1965 until 1982, the DJIA market traded in a narrow range, around 850 plus or minus 100. There were spikes, but they did not last long. The market was seldom above 950 or seldom below 750. Then came the sudden burst upward. In 1982, the DJIA was about 750. Five years later, it was 2800, and at the end of the decade, it was near 3000—a fourfold increase. If you call 1974 the bottom, when the DJIA was below 600, the market was up fivefold. This certainly meets the late Edson Gould's criterion of a classic bull market—a market that is up three to five times from its base.

With a longer life span and longer years in retirement, investors also need the protection of purchasing power that common stocks offer. The RDY discipline responds to this need.

LIFE CYCLE INVESTING

As pointed out when discussing corporate, public, and charitable funds, no one investment approach is right for every institution at every point in its investment life. Nor is there only one right approach for individual investors. There is no need for them, particularly with the proliferation of mutual funds during the 1980s, to be committed to a single style for all of their assets for all of their lives. While the focus of this book is on a particular approach—Relative Dividend Yield—this discipline is not a cure-all or investment equivalent of the universal solvent. Many investors would find it too slow and conservative and would never stick with it. Moreover, there are some times in life when it is perhaps not as appropriate and other times when it is most appropriate.

When you are young, in your twenties and early thirties, you can take a good deal of risk when investing. You could, for example, buy emerging-growth stocks, young and small companies that may well fail but that, if successful, provide very big returns. If the companies do fail, you have many years of career and investing ahead to recover your losses. Also, since you have typically little money to invest at this age anyway, a bit of a "shoot-for-the-moon" attitude may make more sense.

Very often, young people who work for a company that has a 401(k) plan choose the most conservative investment option— usually a guaranteed investment contract that pays a fixed return. The usual advice of financial planners is that these young people are making a mistake, that they should take a more aggressive position, such as one of the equity options. These people may have 30 years or more of investing ahead of them. They can afford to take more risk in the short run since they have the longest time horizons.

The ability of the young to afford risk is true, of course, but it is also important to consider what kinds of accounts are available to bear this risk. For example, if a 401(k) plan is available but an individual has excess funds to invest, it may make more sense to choose an investment alternative that is yield rather than growth oriented for the company plan and to do emerging-growth stock investing independently of the company plan. Some of these higher risk/higher return investments are inevitably not going to work out in the way expected when the investments were made. The losses generated in the more speculative investments can offset income taxes paid from other sources. The U.S. government

141

will bear part of the pain of these mistakes. The same losses would have no tax value within the 401(k) structure.

When you are married and have started a family, the financial picture usually changes radically. Since only one spouse may work after the children arrive, the other not joining in at least for several years, the carefree spending and investing days are over. Mortgage payments and other house-related expenses will probably not leave much money, at least at first, to use for investments. As careers progress, however, with possibly both husband and wife working again, a couple may be able to put aside some money once more. But now, they tend to be far more conservative than during their single and pre-children marriage days. The savings are hard to come by, and the chief objective of these savings is most likely the children's education. At this stage in their lives, the couple may want to minimize the risk of losses. The RDY approach is a very sensible way to achieve the higher return from equities than from fixed-income choices during these years, particularly given the long-term nature of the investment objective.

From their mid-forties until retirement age, many investors typically enjoy their maximum earning years. Money for investments can be systematically set aside. The focus becomes building a nest egg for retirement, even though these investors may still be coping with mortgage and college costs. Stocks are obviously the best passive way—that is, outside of building a business or professional practice—to maximize investment returns. At this stage, people probably feel still young enough, still active enough, still confident enough in the future, to return to a more risk-raking posture. The time horizon is still sufficiently long to contemplate higher-risk investment options within the common stock arena.

As retirement approaches, most individuals start dropping back on this risk level. They do not want to take the risks they took in youth or middle age—when they invested in small, precarious companies. Maturing companies with some growth potential are still, however, a good option.

Then come the immediate pre-retirement and retirement years, when conservatism takes a strong hold—and rightly so. Older people have fewer years left to recover losses. Since they are either retired or soon to retire, they cannot recoup losses through their own labor, and they are never sure they are going to be around on this earth long enough to live through a bear market and participate in the subsequent upswing. Odds are they probably will since people are living longer these days, but, psychologically, they are more aware of their mortality. Most retired people today may be locked into a mix of assets that is not appropriate for their changed circumstances because of the very high capital gains rates currently in place.

In addition to social security and a pension, retirees presumably have some savings. They have to decide how to keep these assets invested to provide the incremental income to live on. Many simply rely on CDs and money market funds, or they roll over 90-day Treasury bills and see their rate of return move up and down with inflation and interest rates. Some buy longer-term bonds and subject themselves to fluctuations in principal value, but at least they lock in a certain income stream over the life of the bonds.

People often turn into financial invalids just because they have reached age 65. They should not, and they do not have to. More time is spent in the retirement years than at any other time in history. Common stocks should still have a part to play at this time of life. *Common stocks, to emphasize the point, have the unique attribute of providing an increasing income stream that can match inflation plus generate appreciation over time.* As people spend a greater portion of their expanding life span in retirement, the ravages of inflation on the purchasing power of their income and accumulated principal must be considered.

If you buy a 30-year Treasury bond and hold it to maturity, you are going to get exactly the same check every six months for the 30 years and the same principal back at maturity. This is the contract you made. And, of course, the purchasing power or value of your principal declines as inflation rises.

Age 70 today is like age 55 forty years ago, and prognostications are that longevity will keep increasing. For their remaining years, most investors should have some exposure to equities. Stocks do better at keeping up with inflation than do savings instruments and other fixed-income options. Even at 3% a year, inflation takes a big bite out of the buying power of assets over time. The longer you

143

live, the longer you have to be concerned about inflation, as well as to ride out market cycles.

The RDY approach is ideal for these years. It gives you an opportunity to earn equity returns but in a more conservative way, with high dividend yields and less severe swings in the value of your portfolio. Psychologically, you will feel as though your investments are more secure than they would be in, say, growth stocks, many of which do not grow as expected. As an RDY investor, you will own big, well-known companies that are no longer fast-growing companies, but their stability will be very reassuring.

Of course, pre-retirees or retirees should not put all of their investable funds in stocks, even though the yield discipline described in this book may seem appropriate. A complete portfolio will have fixed income and cash and possibly real estate. The proportion of each asset will be dictated by the individual's assets, income, and spending needs. For the equity portion of the total portfolio, however, RDY makes a great deal of sense both economically and psychologically.

CHOOSING THE "RIGHT" APPROACH

Aside from the times of life when the RDY approach seems particularly appropriate, the matter of temperament cannot be dismissed. Some people will find the approach appealing at any age. These people will simply see it as "right" for them because they feel more comfortable buying "cheap" stocks, those that look like bargains because they sold at much higher prices in earlier periods. By the same token, they would be uncomfortable owning growth stocks, or bearing the risk of stocks whose growth can stumble. They do not want to bet on growth to come because they know they would have to pay up for it, and there are too many disappointments. Earnings are too unpredictable. The RDY approach, not as dependent on earnings, is simpler and more reliable.

The individual investor has a number of advantages in building a portfolio that is just right for his or her goals and objectives. Still, every investor has to be honest with himself or herself. There is no need to explain a methodology to someone else to get *him or her* to do the right thing. The information available for using the RDY discipline does not require vast amounts of data or great resources of time and money to succeed and to outperform most professionals and other individual investors. The study of the ten highest-yield Dow-Jones Industrial stocks in Appendix A shows what can be done once a year with *Barron's,* the *Wall Street Journal,* or a local newspaper. The RDY graphs in Appendix C can be kept up to date on a quarterly or an annual basis.

In short, the reader of this book who is a private, not institutional, investor must have a good idea of what the issues are in determining his or her own "right" investment approach. The various alternatives have been discussed to further illuminate the importance of matching your needs, goals, and objectives with the right mix of investments and investment styles. You have to be honest with yourself about your strengths and weaknesses and not forget to factor in your own temperament.

If you choose an institution or organization to help you make your investment decisions, you can probably find someone with the right frame of mind to match your needs. When you hire *yourself* to do the job, you have only one choice, and thus you must be truthful about what kind of investor you are.

ADVANTAGES OF CHOOSING THE RDY APPROACH

There are different speeds and different approaches to the market. Traders at heart will not likely succeed in applying disciplines that have proved to take three to five years to implement. Seldom are long-term investors successful in trying to be too smart in the purchase of stocks on a "day-trading" basis. It should be unmistakably clear, moreover, that RDY is not a get-rich-quick recipe. It will not guarantee you 25% a year.

What you do get, however, if you choose to follow RDY investing, is an approach that is logical and proven. It will bring you returns that you can expect from stocks generally—plus a few percentage points more from the higher dividend yield intrinsic to the application of this investment decision process. These extra points, compounded over time, make a tremendous difference in what your original dollars are worth.

Table 9-1 indicates the value of $100,000 compounded monthly over various time periods at differing annual rates of return.

For the individual, as opposed to the tax-exempt institution, the tax rate on both the income and the capital gains has a large influence on the aftertax rate of return. The lower the tax rate, the higher the after-tax rate of return. Given the same style of investing and the same total return, more return coming from capital gains than from income is important if the capital gains tax rate is lower than the tax rate on income.

One of the factors that is underestimated, however, is the impact on after-tax returns of the style of investing used to achieve the returns. Tables 9-2 and 9-3 illustrate the importance of the portfolio and asset turnover rate, which reflect different styles of investment on after-tax return.

Note that the after-tax return is notably higher for low-turnover strategies than for investment policies requiring high turnover even if the tax rate on capital gains is much lower than on income received in the form of a dividend stream.

TABLE 9-1

Value of $100,000 Compounded at Various Rates and Time Periods

Annual Compound Rate of Return	Number of Years			
	5	10	15	25
0%	$100,000	$100,000	$100,000	$100,000
2%	$110,508	$122,120	$134,952	$164,804
4%	$122,100	$149,083	$182,030	$271,377
6%	$134,885	$181,940	$245,409	$446,497
8%	$148,985	$221,964	$330,692	$734,018
10%	$164,531	$270,704	$445,392	$1,205,695
12%	$181,670	$330,039	$599,580	$1,978,847
14%	$200,561	$402,247	$806,751	$3,245,131
16%	$221,381	$490,094	$1,084,974	$5,317,392
18%	$244,322	$596,932	$1,458,437	$8,705,880
20%	$269,597	$726,825	$1,959,500	$14,242,145

TABLE 9-2

Income Tax Rate: 35%; Capital Gains Rate: 35%

% Total Return	Yield %	% Capital Gain	Aftertax Total Return Turnover Rate			
			30%	70%	100%	150%
12.0%	3.0%	9.0%	10.0%	8.7%	7.8%	6.2%
12.0%	4.5%	7.5%	9.6%	8.6%	7.8%	6.5%
12.0%	6.0%	6.0%	9.3%	8.4%	7.8%	6.7%
10.0%	3.0%	7.0%	8.2%	7.2%	6.5%	5.3%
10.0%	4.5%	5.5%	7.8%	7.1%	6.5%	5.5%
10.0%	6.0%	4.0%	7.5%	6.9%	6.5%	5.8%

Using RDY, you will be taking less risk than most professional managers would be taking for you. The longer-term volatility of your total return will also be less than that of the market itself. You will be getting much of your return regularly—in a flow from dividends that at times can be almost twice what most stocks are yielding. Among stock market investment approaches, RDY is

TABLE 9-3

Income Tax Rate: 50%; Capital Gains Rate: 18%

% Total Return	Yield %	% Capital Gain	Aftertax Total Return Turnover Rate			
			30%	70%	100%	150%
12.0%	3.0%	9.0%	10.0%	9.4%	8.9%	8.1%
12.0%	4.5%	7.5%	9.3%	8.8%	8.4%	7.7%
12.0%	6.0%	6.0%	8.7%	8.2%	7.9%	7.4%
10.0%	3.0%	7.0%	8.1%	7.6%	7.2%	6.6%
10.0%	4.5%	5.5%	7.5%	7.1%	6.8%	6.3%
10.0%	6.0%	4.0%	6.8%	6.5%	6.3%	5.9%

conservative. It also may be dull and boring at times but nonetheless effective.

But, as has repeatedly been said, you must have patience with the RDY discipline. Value stocks can take time before enough other investors acknowledge inherent values to subsequently raise the price of the stocks. Under certain market and economic conditions, your portfolio will lag the overall market and other investors. You will read that the market is up sharply and that this or that manager is particularly tuned in and up twice as much as the market. You will hardly ever feel that you just bought the "hot" stocks, although you may have owned them for many a "cold" year. When you do have the "hot" issues in the portfolio, you will not have them for very long since they will not stay cheap and will need to be sold to maintain your discipline. As you sit silent while friends boast about their current big winners, remember that your portfolio will be performing well, achieving above-average total returns and compounding returns slowly and steadily, but seldom in a spectacular way.

But just wait until the market turns down for an extended period of time—it always does. Your portfolio will not go down as much as the market and that of other managers. Over three years, five years, ten years, you will find that you are ahead of most other investors. The RDY portfolio will have outperformed the Dow-Jones Industrial Averages, and you will have endured less risk, less variability of return, and less worry and apprehension.

While the RDY approach forces you to be a "contrarian" at important junctures, you will not be contrarian all of the time, at least not with your total portfolio. Sometimes, it is not appropriate to be contrary, and you must be in the mainstream, owning what Wall Street loves, in order to realize your gains. To get capital appreciation, there are times when you want to be part of the pack. You will find yourself in this position when some of the stocks you own start to benefit from renewed confidence in these companies. Then, when these stocks become so popular that they look expensive based on the RDY discipline and everyone else loves them, you will be contrary again and start selling. Another value of the RDY approach is that in addition to buy and sell areas of valuation, there are also times in between when a "continue-to-hold" position is appropriate.

The RDY approach can most definitely be followed by the individual investor. It will not take hours a day or require a knowledge of higher mathematics, the ability to pore over balance sheets, or the need to make calls to companies' investor relations departments. It will take some attention, of course, which is true even if you allow your money to be handled by a professional manager.

Conclusion

RDY: LOW RISK, HIGH RETURNS

No one investment style or approach is right for every circumstance or works all of the time. The use of RDY does, however, get at the underlying strength and power—or weakness, even frailty—of a company's stock in a way that cuts through most of the investment market's lore and mystique. For the large, maturing companies that are the predominant holdings in most institutional portfolios, RDY simply works better than other approaches do. It promises lower risk and higher returns.

Of course, some other investment approaches can do very well over time. They are difficult, however, for the average institutional or individual investor to apply. Philip Fisher, John Neff, Warren Buffett, and Peter Lynch have achieved superior results over the long term, but the stocks that they use and the analytical techniques that they apply cannot be utilized by most investors.

The RDY approach is not a universal tool. It is not useful for short-term trading or timing. It does not help in picking out the "great growth" companies of the future. It does not discover hidden assets or "story" stocks.

The RDY approach is, however, a different way to look at the investment world. It separates the investor from the emotional whims of the marketplace. Though the levels of attractiveness of most companies do shift over time, in many situations the repetitive swings from love to hate to neglect that characterize the average investor's feelings about a company's stock can readily be identified. Relative Dividend Yield provides a way of looking at these swings with more discipline and enforced patience than do most other valuation methods.

Appendix A

DIVIDEND POWER: A DOW-JONES 30 STOCKS EXERCISE

STOCK SELECTION

A very simple exercise will introduce the power of the dividend as an indicator of stock values. We will look only at the 30 stocks in the Dow-Jones Industrial Average (DJIA), a small group of very well-known companies.

Why do we look at the stocks in the DJIA? It is a group selected by an independent and objective third party. There can be no question of preselection or survivor bias. No one can say that we just picked the stocks that we knew worked. The Dow-Jones company has, in effect, dictated the portfolio. What is more, the Dow-Jones research staff is careful in its selection process. These are leading companies. Corporations that are no longer contributors to economic vitality are removed from the list, as the changes made in May of 1991 indicate. Though the caretakers of the index err on the side of conservatism in deciding changes in its composition, the index, as a portfolio, is not out of date for long.

In this exercise, we look only at *absolute* dividend yield; RDY is not considered. Absolute yield does not work on a broader universe of stocks containing traditionally high-yield stocks like electric utilities, banks, and regional telephone companies, where many of the stocks with the highest absolute yields are similar year after year. The DJIA is still a predominantly industrial-company index, and absolute yield works even though a few stocks appear among the highest-yield stocks quite frequently. As the list becomes more diversified and less industrial, absolute yield may not work as well as it did in the past.

METHODOLOGY

Our study's methodology in working with the year-end dividend yield of the DJIA stocks was as simple as it could be. We considered a 30-year period—the DJIA stocks from the end of 1960 to the end of 1990. Each year, the 30 stocks were ranked by yield and then divided into thirds, groups of ten stocks each, or three "tertiles." We established, then, the ten highest-yielding stocks, or top tertile;

a middle ten; and a lowest ten, or bottom tertile, in terms of yield. Other aspects of our methodology included the following:

- We calculated the absolute dividend yield—the annual dividend rate of each stock divided by its price—for each of the 30 DJIA stocks at each year-end.

- We assumed that on the first day of the new year all stocks were purchased at the year-end closing prices.

- All stocks were equally dollar-weighted and were moved at each year-end into their appropriate tertile.

- All stocks deleted from the index by Dow-Jones during the year were sold at the last closing price just before the deletion, and the proceeds were held in cash until the end of the year.

- Stocks added to the DJIA list were not bought until the beginning of the following year.

- Quarterly dividends were collected and held in cash until year-end.

- All special distributions of stocks and other special payments—most notably, Du Pont's distribution of General Motors stock early in the period—were treated as dividends. The stock received was sold on the first day traded and held as cash until the year-end, as with all dividends.

- We calculated the rates of return of each tertile over one-year holding periods, from the close of one year to the close of the next. Changes in price, year-end to year-end, plus regular and special dividends received, plus any distributions—that is, the total return—were divided by the previous year-end price to provide the rate of return for that year.

- Transaction costs—commissions and market impact—were not considered, but at the same time we did not calculate interest earned on the accumulated dividends and distributions. A dividend received in January was held for the year, but no return was assumed on this cash. The dividend was not reinvested until the beginning of the next year. The interest income earned during the year would have about matched transaction costs.

DIVERSIFICATION

Some stocks have been consistently among the highest absolute-yield stocks. Exxon has been among the top ten highest-yield stocks for 26 out of these 30 years, General Motors for 22, and AT&T for 20. Clearly, these were not always the most attractive stocks to own; you would have had a better indication of this fact if you had looked at *relative,* rather than absolute, yield. Another difficulty in working with absolute yield on the 30 DJIA stocks is that since there have been many years when half of the ten highest-yielding stocks were energy or chemical companies, you ended up with industry concentrations that caused more variability of return than is desirable.

EXTRAORDINARY RESULTS

The outcome of this study was startling. As can be seen from Table A-1, from December 31, 1960, through December 31, 1990,

TABLE A-1

Annualized Results of Dow-Jones Study					
	DJIA as Reported	DJIA Equally Weighted	Yield Tertile		
			Highest	Middle	Lowest
30 years: 1960–1990	10.5%	11.3%	**14.5%**	11.8%	7.6%
Annualized 10 years:					
1980–1990	15.9%	15.2%	**16.4%**	19.5%	9.6%
1970–1980	7.8%	9.8%	**16.7%**	7.5%	5.1%
1960–1970	7.9%	8.9%	**10.2%**	8.5%	8.0%

the annual average compounded total rate of return for the top tertile averaged 14.5% compared with the reported DJIA at 10.5%. (For the equally weighted DJIA, the return would have been slightly higher than for the reported DJIA—11.3%.)

With the most rudimentary decision-making process, the excess return of the top ten highest yielding stocks was substantial—more than 300 basis points above the equally weighted DJIA and 400 basis points above the reported DJIA *each year,* annualized over the 30 years tested.

Cumulative returns—returns linked year to year—were equally dramatic, as can be seen from Table A-2. If you had started out with $100 at the end of 1960 and compounded it at the rates of return realized, by the end of 1990 the DJIA as reported would have turned $100 into $1432. The equally weighted DJIA would have done better, returning $1739. If $100 had been invested in the top tertile every year, it would have turned into $4188.

Standard deviation of return for the reported DJIA was slightly higher than the equally weighted DJIA–16.2% versus 15.9%—as can be seen from Table A-3. It was very similar for the top tertile— 16.0%. Even higher volatility in the top tertile would have been expected, given the slight diversification among the ten stocks. In many years, as was pointed out, one or two industry groups dominated the portfolio. There was not enough diversification to pro-

TABLE A-2

Cumulative Results of Dow-Jones Study

| | DJIA as Reported | DJIA Equally Weighted | Yield Tertile | | |
			Highest	Middle	Lowest
30 years to 1990	1432%	1739%	**4188%**	2110%	485%
10 years:					
1980–1990	408%	380%	**428%**	546%	222%
1970–1980	179%	217%	**417%**	178%	123%
1960–1970	196%	218%	**240%**	210%	202%

TABLE A-3

Standard Deviation of Return for Dow-Jones Study

	DJIA as Reported	DJIA Equally Weighted	Yield Tertile		
			Highest	Middle	Lowest
30 years: 1960–1990	16.2%	15.9%	**16.0%**	16.3%	18.6%
10 years: 1980–1990	13.4%	13.8%	**13.2%**	14.8%	16.7%
1970–1980	19.4%	19.4%	**18.5%**	18.0%	24.3%
1960–1970	13.7%	12.9%	**14.9%**	12.9%	12.7%

vide the countervailing movement you would have had, for example, if you had owned a broader universe of stocks with a different investment process such as RDY.

Note: No assumption about effective taxes was made in the study. Obviously, returns could be substantially different for a tax-liable investor, depending on the actual turnover from one tertile to another. The power of compounded dividend yield is particularly beneficial to tax-exempt pension plans, both defined-benefit and 401(k) and other defined-contribution plans, as well as Keoghs, IRAs, and rollovers.

In short, the process could not be simpler: You know nothing more about the stocks you buy than their dividend rate at the end of the year. You could make other fundamental judgments—for example, decide that what you had read about asbestos meant that you should not own Manville—but forget all such judgmental add-ons to the strategy, and it still works.

COMPOUNDING INCOME AND STOCK VALUATION

Why does the process work? First, there is the power of compounding the dividends of stocks having a yield that is substantially higher than the average for the DJIA. This alone gives investors an edge over the market. Second, high dividend yield tends to point to the stocks that are the cheapest of the 30. These are the stocks that are out of favor, those with prices so beaten down that their dividends make them the highest-yielding stocks.

In a few instances, dividend increases alone placed stocks among the top tertile, but the usual pattern was that the stocks had fallen out of favor in the marketplace and the stocks dropped in price. (A discussion of yield and relative yield change is found in Appendix B.) This is very clear, for example, in the case of both Eastman Kodak and IBM, each of which appeared among the top ten only within the last couple of years. Although some names were recurrent, there was enough rotation to provide the desired results.

The stocks that moved into the top ten dropped in price until they were cheap. The earnings of many of these companies were disappointing. Investors therefore shunned them, forcing down prices. The dividend, however, was firm, raising the yield. The dividends of these large, maturing companies reflect the deliberations of highly qualified managements and boards of directors. DJIA companies have access to the best investment bankers and staff to analyze future earnings prospects and make sound judgments on appropriate dividend levels. *The dividend is a proportion of normal, sustainable, trend earnings*—an important point that most investors miss.

Some of the stocks in the top ten cut their dividends while their stocks were in the top ten. This statistical review included all of these instances. For example, during the early months of 1991, two of the stocks in the top tertile, General Motors and Goodyear Tire, cut their dividends. If the cuts had been made at year-end 1990, they were significant enough that they would have excluded these two stocks from the top tertile in 1991.

IMPORTANT LESSONS

Interestingly, in the last ten years, the middle tertile performed best. As Table A-1 indicates, the reported DJIA was up, on an annual average compounded basis, 15.9%, and the equally weighted DJIA was about the same—15.2%. Both had virtually the same standard deviation of return (see Table A-3), about 13%;

the 1980s were much less volatile than the 1970s. The top tertile beat the DJIA slightly. It was up 16.4% annually, on average, and the variability of returns was slightly lower—13.0%. The return of the middle tertile, however, was 19.5%, and the volatility, 14.8%, was only slightly higher than that of the DJIA.

Why did the middle tertile do better in the 1980s? One of the reasons for the better showing of the middle group in the 1980s may be the influx of investment money from abroad. Japanese investors, in particular, wanted big-name, safe stocks. The top-tertile stocks had high dividend yields because their prices had fallen, which in turn was due to some perceived problems. The Japanese investors avoided companies with problems. The low yields of the bottom-tertile stocks, on the other hand, often reflected cuts in dividends or even eliminations of dividends; these companies were in greater trouble. Thus, the middle group benefited. The lowest tertile had returns of only 12.6% and above-market variability of 15.5%.

For the full 30 years, however, the middle tertile, not surprisingly, gave investors returns closer to that of the market—though somewhat higher, 12.3%—with a standard deviation of return about the same as that of the DJIA. In cumulative returns, the middle tertile returned $2230 versus $1795 for the equally weighted DJIA.

The real loser was the third tertile. Its annual average return was a mere 7.5%, and the standard deviation of return was higher—18.8%. By the time a stock is mature enough to be admitted into the DJIA, it is not likely to be a dynamic growth stock any longer. Without this growth in earnings, it needs to have a high yield to interest investors. There are admittedly exceptions: Procter & Gamble has been in the DJIA for the whole period, and Coca-Cola and McDonald's are more recent additions. It is likely that McDonald's will be less of a growth stock over the next ten years than it was over the previous ten years largely because of its size and market saturation.

Many of the low-yield stocks have cut or eliminated their dividends, a sure sign of fundamental problems that may eventually cause their elimination from the index. The odds against the ten stocks with the lowest yields doing better than the market is very, very low. This is another important lesson of this exercise. Although some growth stocks, such as Digital Equipment or Federal Express, that pay *no* dividend, did fantastically well in the time period under consideration, growth stocks need to grow, since there is little or no dividend support when problems occur.

Some people have commented that high-yield investing has done well recently due to the merger and acquisition mania of the 1980s and due to the decline in interest rates. The 1980s were not, however, the great period for yield investing; high-yield stocks did far better in the 1970s compared with the other stocks in the DJIA as shown in Table A-1. In fact, it was the glory decade for such stocks, a decade when interest rates were skyrocketing and there was not much in the way of merger and LBO activity. The reported DJIA returned only 7.8% and the equally weighted DJIA, 9.8%, while the top-tertile number was up 16.7% per year during the 1970s. As a result of the Nifty Fifty/Tier I mania of the early 1970s, many of the growth stocks in the DJIA had become badly over-priced. Another reason for the DJIA's poor overall market perfor-mance may have been that a number of bottom-tertile stocks had cut their dividends and were in serious trouble. The Dow-Jones committee had to eventually remove several names from the index.

Conversely, perhaps the reason that high-yield investing was so successful in the 1970s was that it was a decade of turmoil, with a severe worldwide recession in the middle years and then growing inflation and catastrophic governmental economic policies in re-sponse. When in distress, people usually hide in yield stocks. They say to themselves, "I don't understand what's going on, but at least I'm collecting the dividend, even if there is some risk."

The 1960s were quite average, and the 1990s will probably look more like the 1960s than like the other two decades. The top tertile provided only a 10.2% return, but this was still substantially better than the DJIA, as reported or as equally weighted. The standard deviation was higher, however, the result of stocks like Chrysler, which did horribly in 1966, then made a spectacular comeback the following year.

THE NECESSITY OF A LONG-TERM PERSPECTIVE

It is important to note that, as shown in Table A-4, the top tertile did not beat the DJIA and the other tertiles each and every year.

TABLE A-4

Annual Returns of Dow-Jones Study

One Year		DJIA as	DJIA Equally	Yield Tertile		
From	To	Reported	Weighted	Highest	Middle	Lowest
1989	1990	− 0.5%	− 7.9%	− 7.6%	− 5.8%	−10.2%
1988	1989	30.5%	28.4%	22.4%	32.7%	30.0%
1987	1988	15.5%	16.3%	22.1%	18.4%	8.3%
1986	1987	5.8%	14.4%	4.8%	15.1%	23.2%
1985	1986	26.6%	17.8%	25.2%	26.9%	1.3%
1984	1985	32.5%	29.9%	27.7%	37.8%	24.1%
1983	1984	0.6%	− 0.3%	6.4%	2.0%	− 9.2%
1982	1983	25.5%	34.4%	38.6%	31.6%	33.2%
1981	1982	26.0%	21.6%	20.7%	34.2%	9.9%
1980	1981	− 3.6%	− 3.0%	4.0%	1.8%	−14.9%
1979	1980	21.1%	21.8%	27.6%	18.7%	19.0%
1978	1979	10.1%	14.9%	11.8%	23.4%	9.5%
1977	1978	2.3%	− 2.4%	− 2.4%	1.7%	− 6.4%
1976	1977	−13.3%	− 9.2%	7.4%	−16.8%	−18.2%
1975	1976	22.3%	30.8%	34.8%	28.1%	29.5%
1974	1975	44.5%	47.6%	58.9%	37.3%	46.6%
1973	1974	−23.5%	−17.4%	− 1.7%	−14.6%	−36.0%
1972	1973	−13.5%	−10.9%	3.4%	−12.7%	−23.4%
1971	1972	18.1%	15.5%	23.2%	8.2%	15.1%
1970	1971	9.9%	6.8%	3.8%	1.2%	15.4%
1969	1970	9.1%	10.7%	8.1%	11.6%	12.4%
1968	1969	−11.9%	−10.1%	−14.1%	− 9.7%	− 6.5%
1967	1968	7.8%	9.4%	11.8%	15.6%	0.9%
1966	1967	19.1%	21.9%	26.7%	19.8%	19.1%
1965	1966	−15.9%	−15.4%	−18.8%	−14.6%	−12.9%
1964	1965	14.2%	16.6%	17.4%	18.5%	13.7%
1963	1964	17.7%	18.0%	20.8%	19.5%	13.8%
1962	1963	21.7%	21.0%	20.6%	13.4%	29.0%
1961	1962	− 6.7%	− 2.8%	4.9%	− 7.6%	− 5.6%
1960	1961	23.6%	20.1%	25.0%	18.6%	16.6%

The top tertile was the best performer among the three only half of the time—15 out of the 30 years. In 10 of the years, it ranked second in performance; in 5 of them, it was actually the worst performing of the three groups. The top tertile beat the market—as opposed to the other two tertiles—19 out of the 30 years. In the 1980s, the top tertile did better than the market only 5 out of the 10 years. In 1990, there was such a large difference between the price change of the reported DJIA and the price change of the average stock in the index that the top tertile failed to beat either the market or the middle tertile, but did do better than the equally weighted DJIA. See Figure A-1.

High-yield investing, in general, including RDY investing, is not an investment approach that will win every week, every month, every quarter, or even every year. It is when the market is not doing particularly well that high-yield stocks in the top tertile really shine. Furthermore, when the top tertile does better than the market, it does much better; when it performs worse than the market, it performs only a little worse. In a bull market period

FIGURE A-1

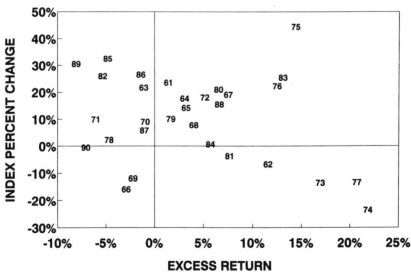

Excess Return of Top Tertile DJIA as Reported

like the 1980s, it may not perform as well, and yet the rates of return are still very high.

Even the lowest-yield stocks beat the DJIA every once in a while—8 out of the 30 years. Not only did they not do it often, but it was not by very much. In many of these "good" years, the lowest tertile was not the best performing of the three groups. When the lowest-yield tertile did poorly, it did very poorly. The worst performing years, when there were very large low or negative excess returns, occurred in strong market years as well as in weak market years. Note 1973, when the market was down about 25% and the lowest tertile of yield was off 12% more than this. See Figure A-2.

As would be expected, the middle tertile, on average, provided fairly close to market returns across good and bad years. There were time periods when it was better and others when it was worse. There was no consistent pattern of performing better—or worse—than the DJIA in advancing years.

When you compare the returns of the ten highest-yielding stocks

FIGURE A-2

Excess Return of Low Tertile DJIA as Reported

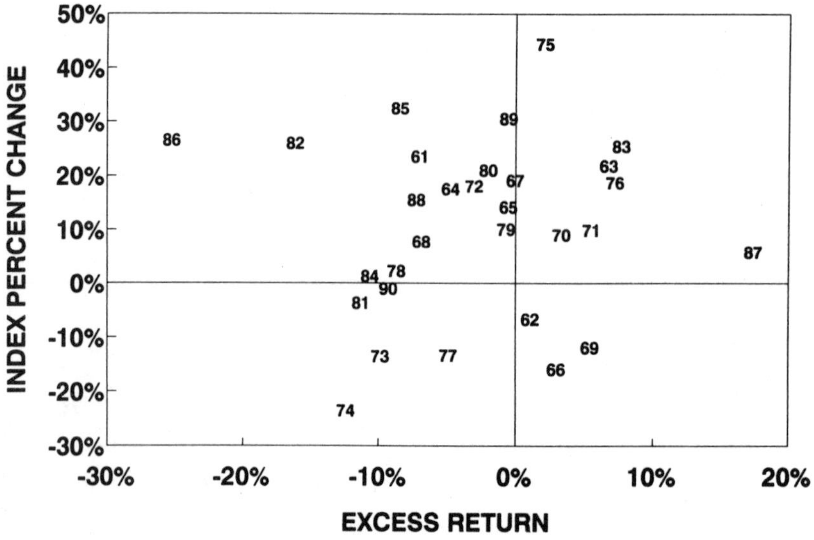

with the DJIA year by year, you find a consistent pattern: They did better in more years, and they did considerably better. When the market was off 20%, the top tertile's excess return was plus 20%. Thus, the absolute return was 0%, and a zero return when the market did so badly is a very, very good result.

There were many instances when the market's return was negative and the top tertile turned in a positive excess return. The year with the largest negative excess return was when the absolute return on the DJIA was very high. In 1989, the DJIA was up 30% and the top tertile was up only 22%. But the downside protection— the very high excess returns in years when the market was off sharply—along with the ability to about match the market in some years and perform somewhat better in others more than made up for the occasions when absolute rates of return for the DJIA were unusually high.

THE DIVIDEND DIFFERENTIAL

In summation, the Dow-Jones 30 exercise was rather amazing: Every year, the ten highest-yielding stocks in the DJIA were bought and then held for a year. Simple rules applied to an independent universe of stocks implemented just once a year. Yet, the average return for the 30 years ending December 31, 1990, was 14.5% compared with 10.5% for the reported DJIA and 11.3% for the equally weighted DJIA. A sum of $100 turned into $4188 instead of the reported DJIA's $1432. The standard deviation of return was about the same as that of the DJIA. In short, you had higher return with equal variability.

The fact that high dividend yields point out the best values among the Dow-Jones stocks suggests another consideration—that high yield in and of itself is attractive since every investor must think in terms of total return. If two stocks among a group of long-established industrial companies like those in the DJIA had about the same growth rate, balance sheet strength, industry attractiveness, and so on, but one had a 3% yield and the other a 5% yield, would you not always want to pick up the 200 additional basis points in total return because of the higher current income? When you get down to the lowest common denominator, stocks with higher yields command authority. Of course, stocks differ in growth rates and the rest, but over long enough time horizons all big companies begin to look very much alike. The dividend yield then becomes a way to differentiate one from another to decide which is more attractive among stocks with similar earnings growth rates.

WHY USING RDY MAKES SENSE

Why, then, you well might ask, bother to use *Relative Dividend Yield*? Even if the returns of the RDY and Dow-Jones disciplines were similar, many practical considerations tell against the Dow-Jones study approach. How many institutional investors, for example, would be comfortable owning only ten stocks in a $100 million portfolio? Nor should investors accept such a mechanical way of stock selection; a fiduciary should want to know something about the companies in which his or her institution has invested money. Analysis of companies reduces the number of mistakes since cash flows, balance sheet strength, and dividend-paying culture add to the safety and certainty of the dividends being paid.

Absolute yield does not discriminate between good and bad times to own many high-yield stocks. A more discriminating valuation method would have indicated when it was advisable to have owned Exxon or General Motors, times when other choices offered higher probability of success, even though these stocks were still in the top tertile of yield. Moreover, many stocks that would have been good stocks to own for most of the period never had high enough absolute yields to be in the top tertile.

Equally important, *RDY-disciplined returns are far better on a risk-adjusted basis* because broader industry participation provides better diversification and lowers volatility and risk. By considering a broader universe of stocks and looking at RDY, the investor can achieve lower variability of return and better performance. As has been shown, with the highest tertile of yield among the Dow-Jones stocks, you end up with fairly severe industry concentrations. Half of the ten can be in the chemicals and oils. Since the oils usually

166

have important chemical divisions, when chemicals do badly, five out of your ten stocks are weak performers. There are also times when industrials do not do as well as electric utilities or financial stocks, which are little represented in the DJIA. Consequently, the RDY investor achieves a much lower risk level by virtue of industry and company diversification, while still earning returns equal to or better than that of the market and the top tertile of the DJIA.

Appendix B

**DIVIDEND YIELD
AND YIELD CHANGE**

The research conducted for this study looked at change in dividend yield over various time periods and the total returns achieved over various subsequent holding periods. This data has confirmed the value of looking at changes in dividend yield as a basic valuation technique aimed at identifying value in unpopular stocks and selling positions in these stocks as they become too popular. The statistical work was first published in the spring 1990 issue of the *Journal of Portfolio Management* (JPM) using a "survivors only" data base. An extension of the work covering an "as was" data base was presented at the fall 1990 meeting of the Institute for Quantitative Investments, or "Q Group." This research confirms the low-volatility nature of the change-in-yield approach and generates holding periods typically in the three-to-five-year range for a turnover of 25% to 30% per year. It also reinforces the thesis that the approach works on the stocks of large companies with above-market yields but does not work with smaller companies and low-yield stocks. An increase in yield for small companies with high-yield stocks may reflect true company fundamental problems rather than the fact that the stocks are out of favor and unpopular as may be the case with large, high-yield stocks.

There are many explanations as to why the change-in-yield approach works. It may reflect no more than the phenomenon that falling stock prices tend to be followed by rising prices. But price rebound alone accounts for only a portion of the generation of excess returns. The reasons behind the higher yield, however, offer the opportunity for analysts to review the fundamentals and decide whether the lower price might reflect temporary problems or more permanent problems that might cause the dividend to be cut. The use of dividend yield as a basic valuation technique supplies something that no other approach (price/earnings, price-to-book value, or market capitalization/revenue) offers—a comparison with other sources of income and total return from bonds, other stocks, or cash.

During the many years that we have been applying RDY relative yield change as a valuation technique, we have thought that the dividend represented a payout percentage of "normal" or sustainable earnings power. Reported earnings for most companies give a very unreliable method of valuation. Stocks with earnings cyclicality or that have earnings problems typically sell at their highest price/earnings multiples when their prices are depressed. When reported earnings are strong and the company is doing well, the multiples are lower.

Dividend policy at most large corporations is taken very seriously by managements and boards of directors. Changes in the dividend are not done without considerable review of the longer-term fundamentals of a company and the industry within which it must operate. Just as the oil companies did not raise dividends as much as earnings increased in the late 1970s when oil prices were escalating and profit margins reached very high levels, so they did not cut dividends in the mid-1980s when product prices dropped sharply and earnings plunged. Again, our use of dividends provides the same information that "normal earnings" P/Es would provide, but in a much more direct manner. The use of dividends does not require the arbitrary choice of time periods to be averaged to arrive at normal earnings, nor does it require assumptions about future profit margins and sales levels.

In addition to providing a discipline that aims at removing the emotionalism of the marketplace, the income stream itself is an important source of an addition to total return. While yields are volatile, moving up and down with price, the income stream has been a reliable source of return that grows over time.

The data base used for the Q Group presentation reinforced the thoughts in the JPM article, which contained neither bankrupt companies nor those that have been acquired. This further research indicated there is no survivor bias in the data base used for the JPM paper.

Appendix C

**RDY CHARTS
FOR THE INVESTOR**

This section contains a series of RDY graphs of major companies that have qualified, do qualify, or may qualify for an RDY portfolio over the next five years. Since there will probably be close to 200 names that may come in and out of investor favor over the next five years, this is clearly just a sample. Room has been left on each chart for the reader to plot RDY in the future. The graphs contain data based on month-end prices, plotted four times per year. This information provides an idea of the basic under- and overvaluation periods for each of these companies.

Also included are the current buy and sell levels for each of these companies. The minimum beginning buy point for any stock qualifying for the RDY discipline is 100%—that is, a yield equal to that of the market. Some of these stocks may not reach this level during the next five years. Just because a stock's yield is low does not mean that it will not do well in the market. For all of these large companies, however, earnings growth must continue to match or exceed current expectations, or the yields are likely to rise to a point where they are attractive to the RDY investor.

This appendix has all of the 25 stocks listed in the sample portfolio in Chapter 7, as well as 30 other well-known stocks. These stocks are possible candidates that should be followed during the next five to ten years.

FIGURE C-1

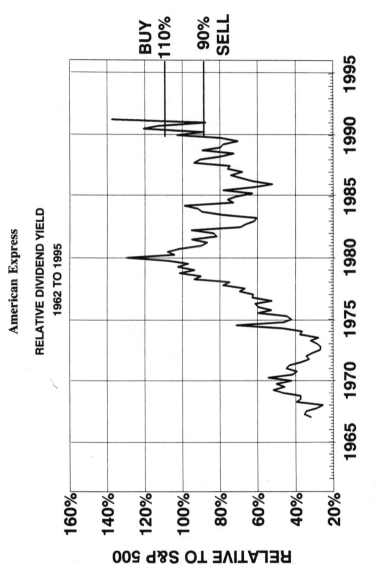

American Express

RELATIVE DIVIDEND YIELD
1962 TO 1995

QUARTERLY OBSERVATIONS ARE IN MAR, JUN, SEPT & DEC

175

FIGURE C-2

Amoco Corporation

RELATIVE DIVIDEND YIELD

1962 TO 1995

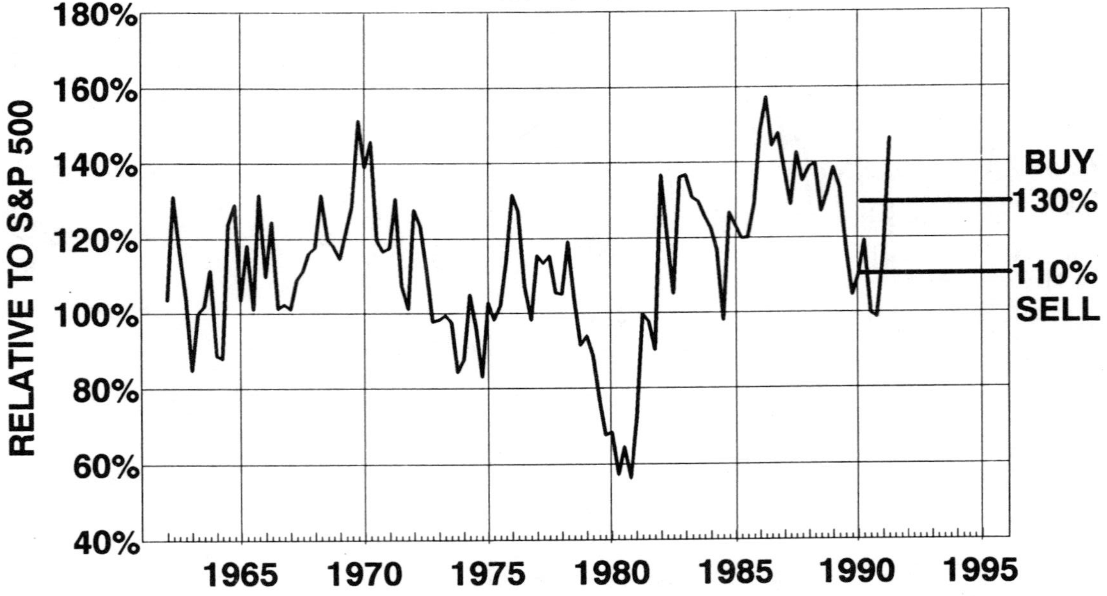

QUARTERLY OBSERVATIONS ARE IN MAR, JUN, SEPT & DEC

176

FIGURE C-3

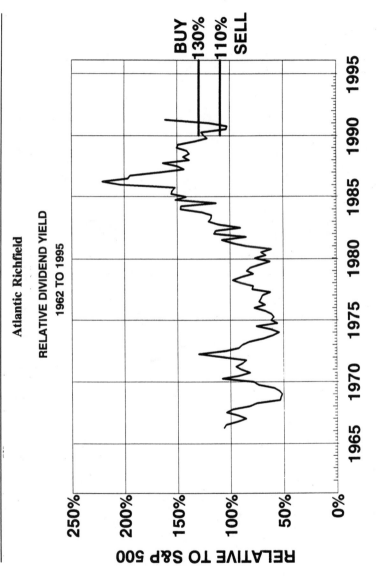

Atlantic Richfield

RELATIVE DIVIDEND YIELD
1962 TO 1995

QUARTERLY OBSERVATIONS ARE IN MAR, JUN, SEPT & DEC

177

FIGURE C-4

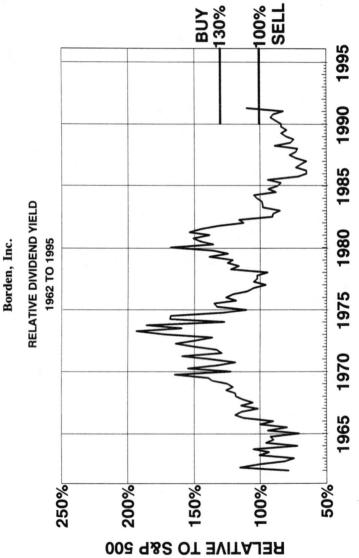

Borden, Inc.

RELATIVE DIVIDEND YIELD
1962 TO 1995

QUARTERLY OBSERVATIONS ARE IN MAR, JUN, SEPT & DEC

FIGURE C-5

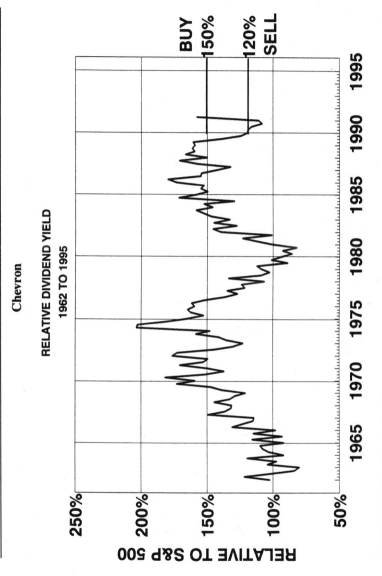

Chevron

RELATIVE DIVIDEND YIELD
1962 TO 1995

BUY
150%

120%
SELL

250%

200%

150%

100%

50%

RELATIVE TO S&P 500

1965   1970   1975   1980   1985   1990   1995

QUARTERLY OBSERVATIONS ARE IN MAR, JUN, SEPT & DEC

179

FIGURE C-6

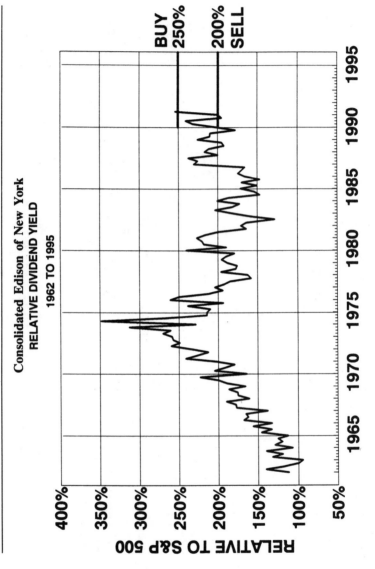

Consolidated Edison of New York
RELATIVE DIVIDEND YIELD
1962 TO 1995

QUARTERLY OBSERVATIONS ARE IN MAR, JUN, SEPT & DEC

FIGURE C-7

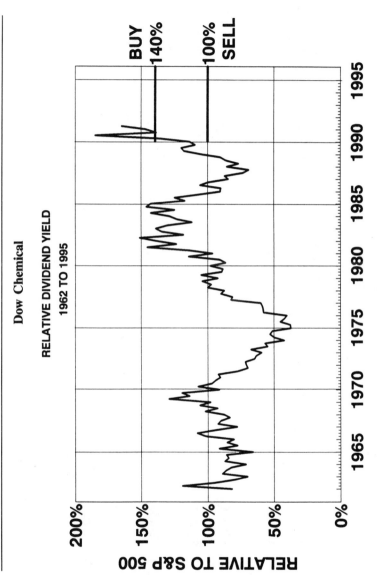

Dow Chemical

RELATIVE DIVIDEND YIELD
1962 TO 1995

QUARTERLY OBSERVATIONS ARE IN MAR, JUN, SEPT & DEC

181

FIGURE C-8

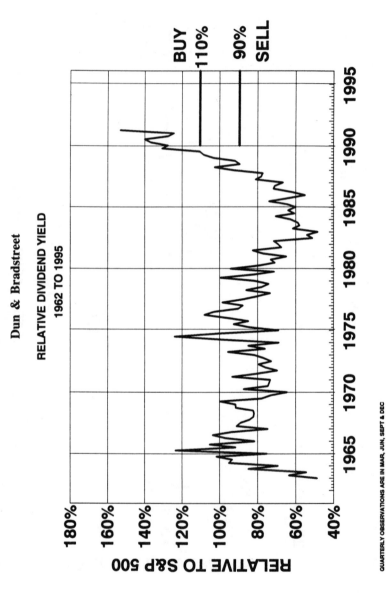

Dun & Bradstreet

RELATIVE DIVIDEND YIELD
1962 TO 1995

QUARTERLY OBSERVATIONS ARE IN MAR, JUN, SEPT & DEC

FIGURE C-9

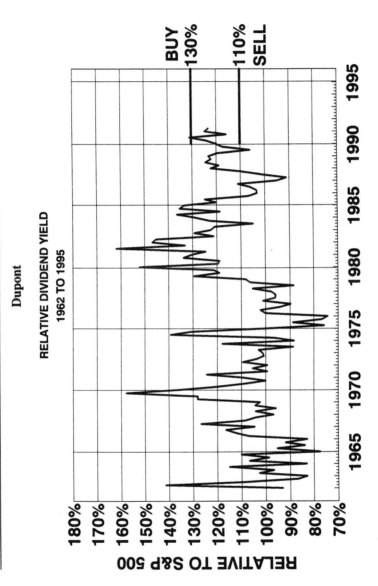

Dupont

RELATIVE DIVIDEND YIELD
1962 TO 1995

QUARTERLY OBSERVATIONS ARE IN MAR, JUN, SEPT & DEC

183

FIGURE C-10

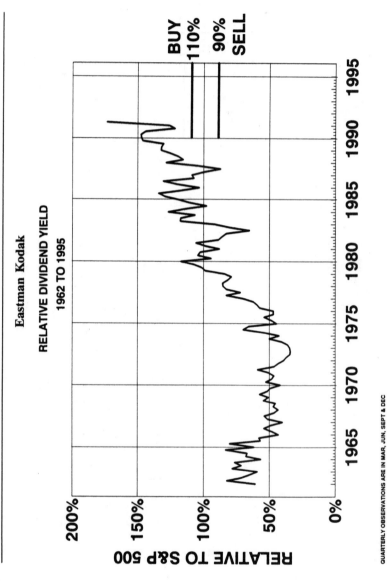

Eastman Kodak

RELATIVE DIVIDEND YIELD

1962 TO 1995

RELATIVE TO S&P 500

200%   150%   100%   50%   0%

1965   1970   1975   1980   1985   1990   1995

BUY
110%
90%
SELL

QUARTERLY OBSERVATIONS ARE IN MAR, JUN, SEPT & DEC

184

FIGURE C-11

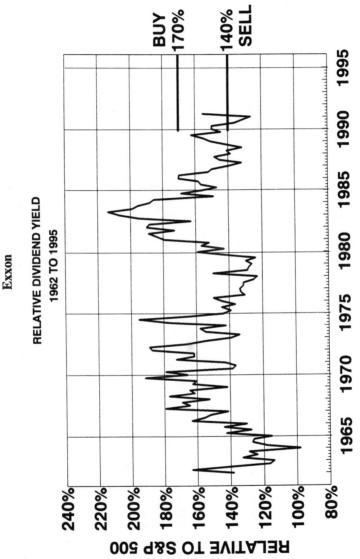

Exxon

RELATIVE DIVIDEND YIELD
1962 TO 1995

QUARTERLY OBSERVATIONS ARE IN MAR, JUN, SEPT & DEC

FIGURE C-12

Ford

RELATIVE DIVIDEND YIELD
1962 TO 1995

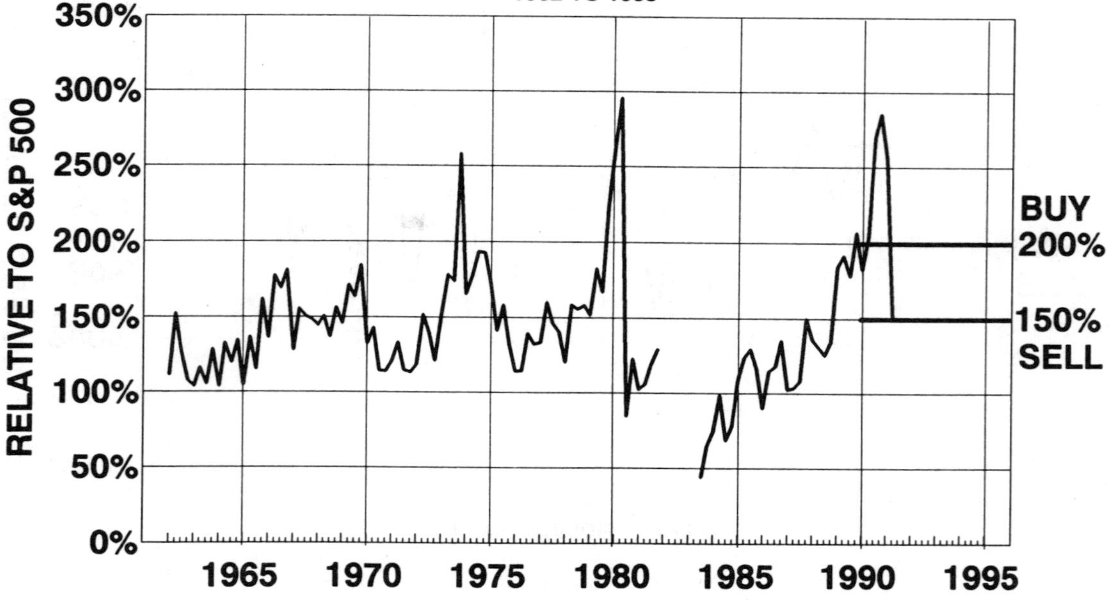

QUARTERLY OBSERVATIONS ARE IN MAR, JUN, SEPT & DEC

FIGURE C-13

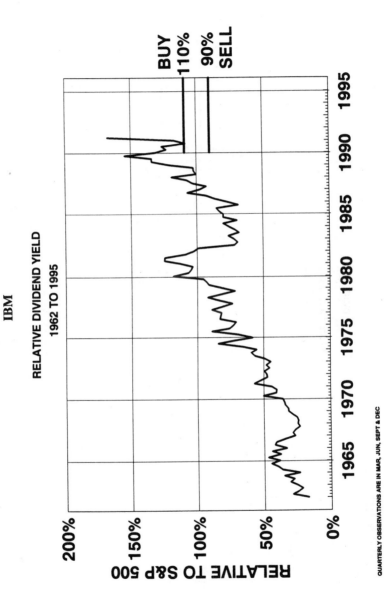

IBM

RELATIVE DIVIDEND YIELD
1962 TO 1995

QUARTERLY OBSERVATIONS ARE IN MAR, JUN, SEPT & DEC

FIGURE C-14

Kmart

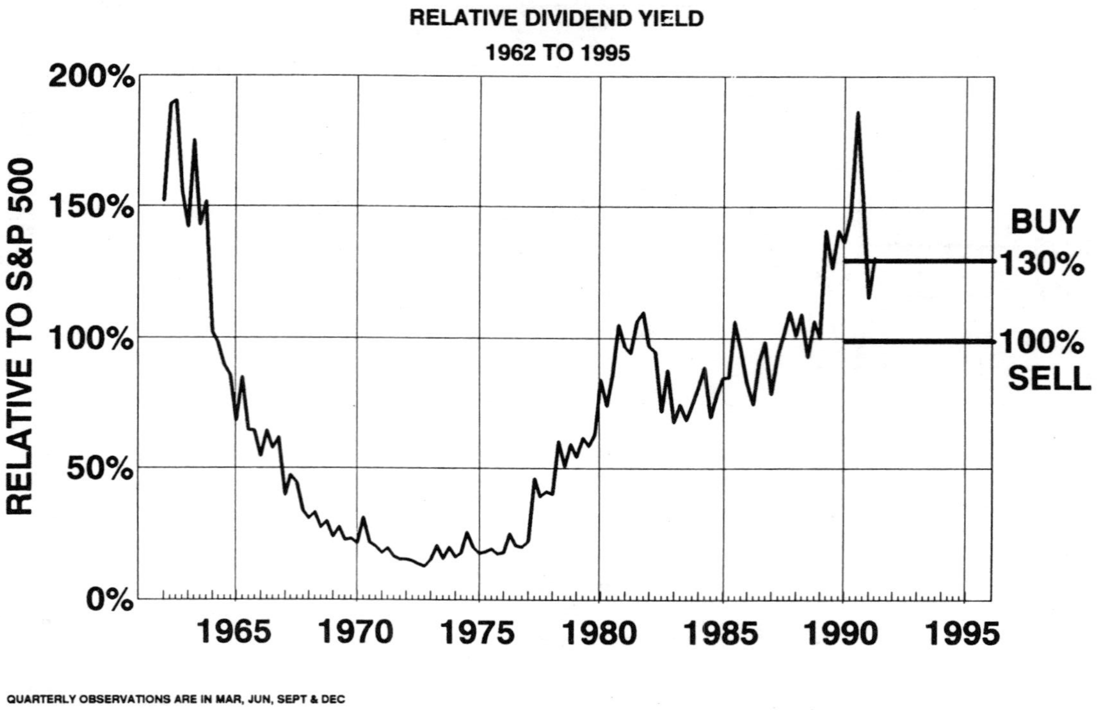

RELATIVE DIVIDEND YIELD
1962 TO 1995

QUARTERLY OBSERVATIONS ARE IN MAR, JUN, SEPT & DEC

188

FIGURE C-15

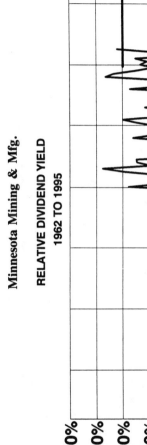
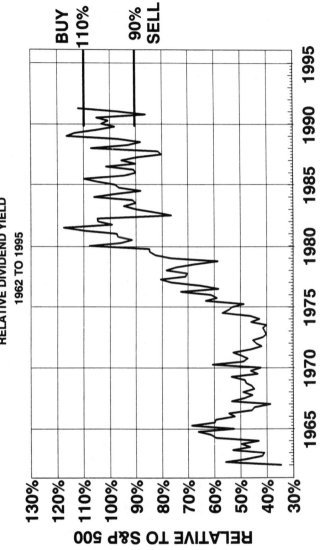

Minnesota Mining & Mfg.

RELATIVE DIVIDEND YIELD
1962 TO 1995

QUARTERLY OBSERVATIONS ARE IN MAR, JUN, SEPT & DEC

189

FIGURE C-16

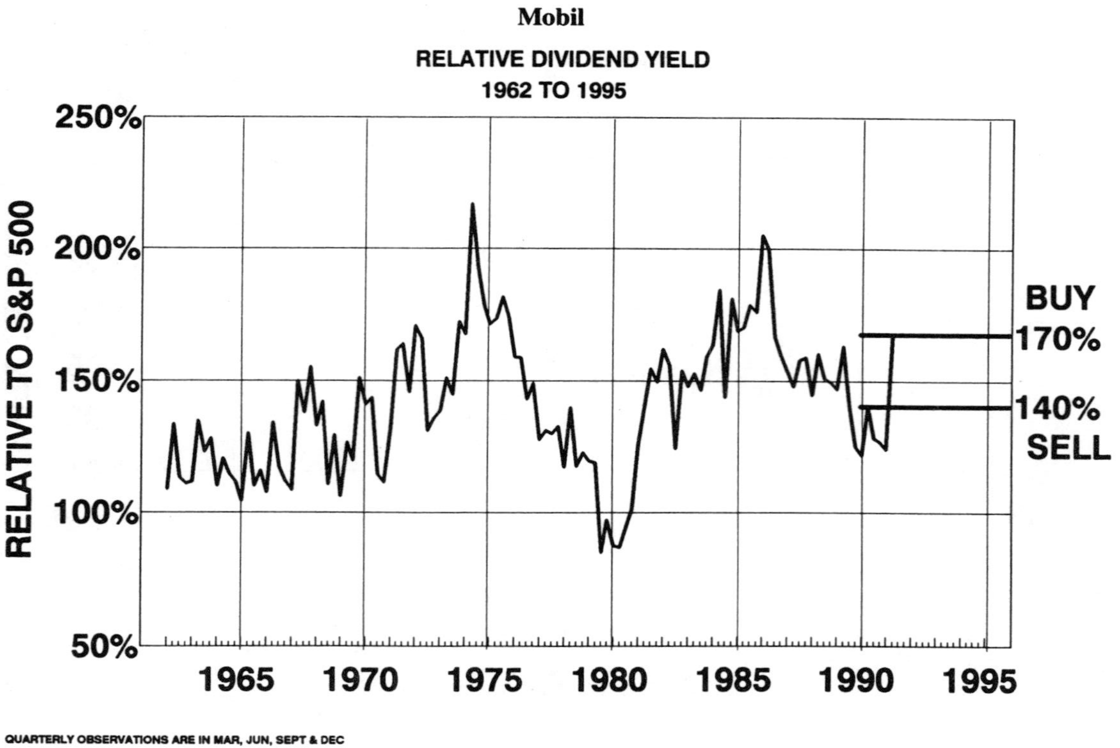

Mobil

RELATIVE DIVIDEND YIELD
1962 TO 1995

QUARTERLY OBSERVATIONS ARE IN MAR, JUN, SEPT & DEC

190

FIGURE C-17

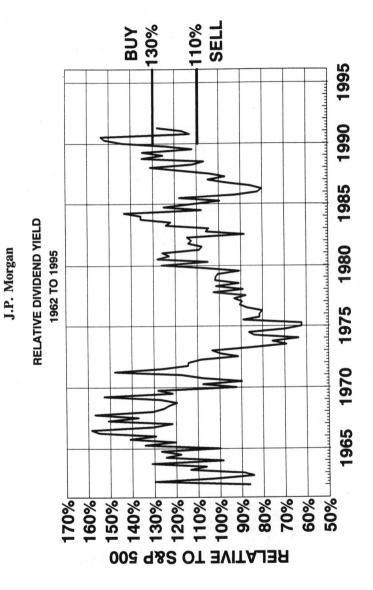

J.P. Morgan

RELATIVE DIVIDEND YIELD
1962 TO 1995

QUARTERLY OBSERVATIONS ARE IN MAR, JUN, SEPT & DEC

191

FIGURE C-18

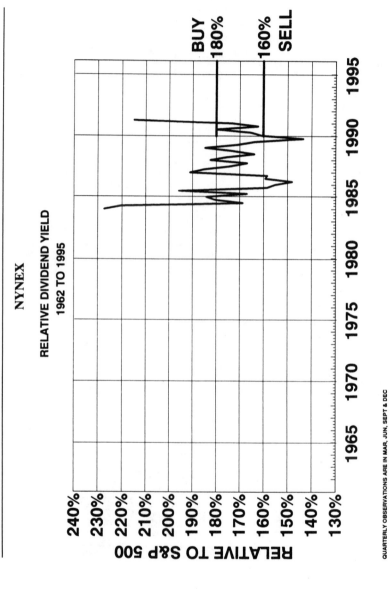

NYNEX

RELATIVE DIVIDEND YIELD
1962 TO 1995

QUARTERLY OBSERVATIONS ARE IN MAR, JUN, SEPT & DEC

FIGURE C-19

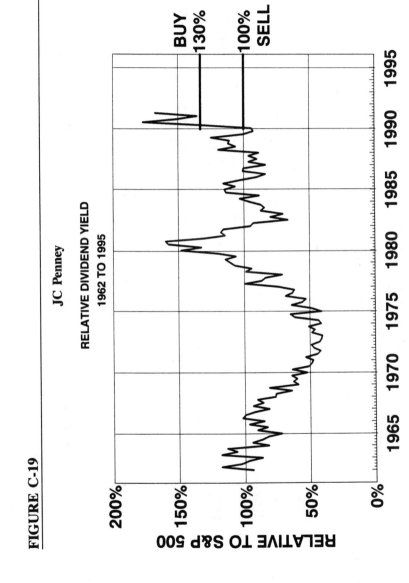

JC Penney

RELATIVE DIVIDEND YIELD
1962 TO 1995

QUARTERLY OBSERVATIONS ARE IN MAR, JUN, SEPT & DEC

193

FIGURE C-20

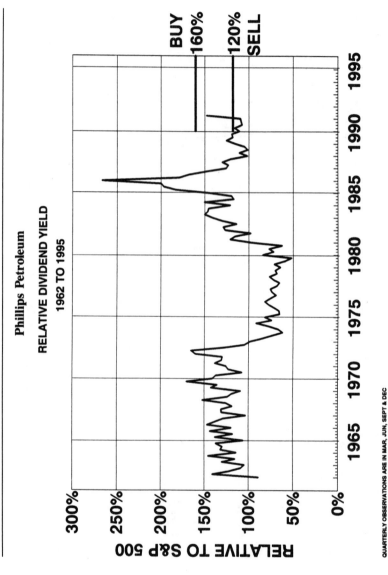

Phillips Petroleum

RELATIVE DIVIDEND YIELD

1962 TO 1995

QUARTERLY OBSERVATIONS ARE IN MAR, JUN, SEPT & DEC

194

FIGURE C-21

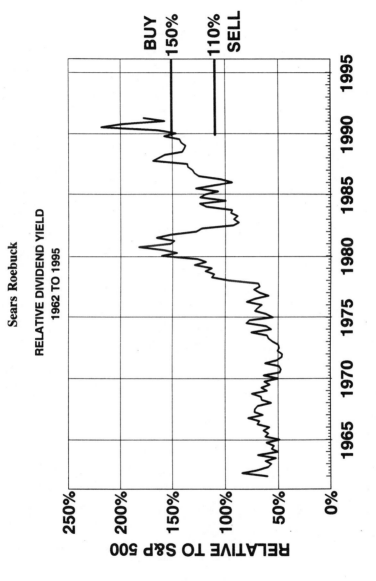

Sears Roebuck

RELATIVE DIVIDEND YIELD
1962 TO 1995

BUY
150%

110%
SELL

RELATIVE TO S&P 500

250%
200%
150%
100%
50%
0%

1965 1970 1975 1980 1985 1990 1995

QUARTERLY OBSERVATIONS ARE IN MAR, JUN, SEPT & DEC

195

FIGURE C-22

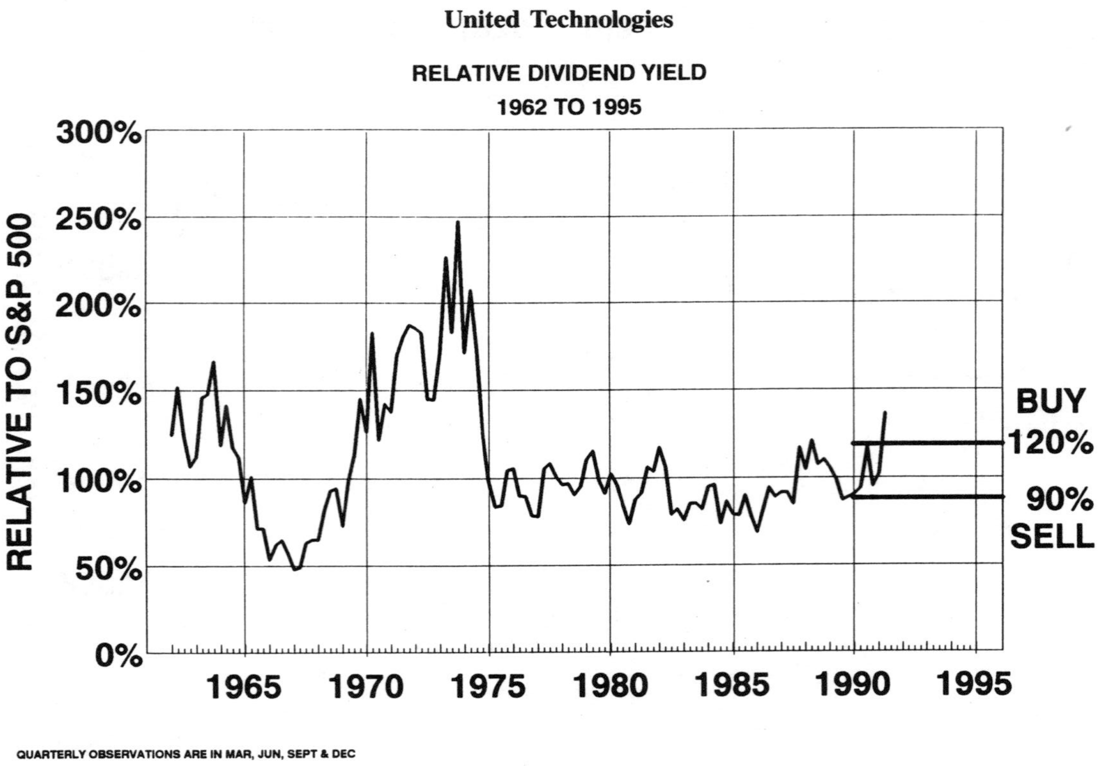
United Technologies
RELATIVE DIVIDEND YIELD
1962 TO 1995
RELATIVE TO S&P 500
300%
250%
200%
150%
100%
50%
0%
1965
1970
1975
1980
1985
1990
1995
BUY
120%
90%
SELL
QUARTERLY OBSERVATIONS ARE IN MAR, JUN, SEPT & DEC

FIGURE C-23

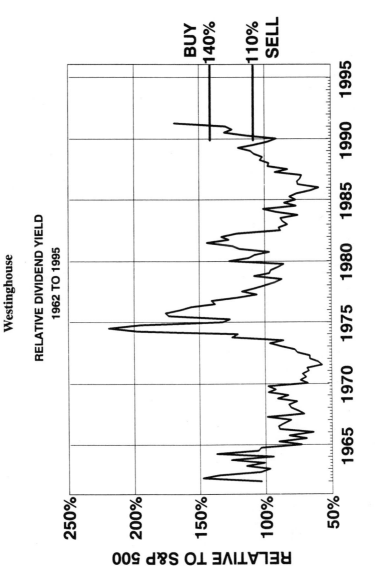

Westinghouse

RELATIVE DIVIDEND YIELD
1962 TO 1995

BUY
140%
110%
SELL

RELATIVE TO S&P 500

250%
200%
150%
100%
50%

1965 1970 1975 1980 1985 1990 1995

QUARTERLY OBSERVATIONS ARE IN MAR, JUN, SEPT & DEC

197

FIGURE C-24

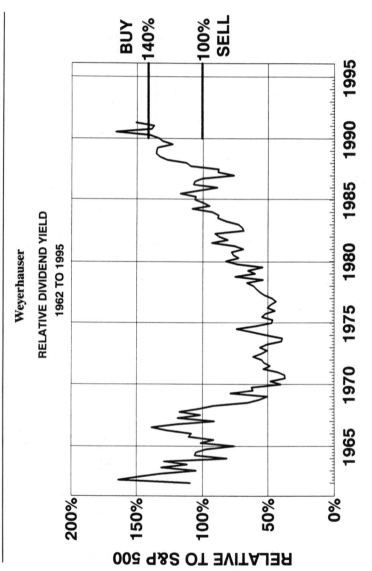

Weyerhauser

RELATIVE DIVIDEND YIELD

1962 TO 1995

QUARTERLY OBSERVATIONS ARE IN MAR, JUN, SEPT & DEC

FIGURE C-25

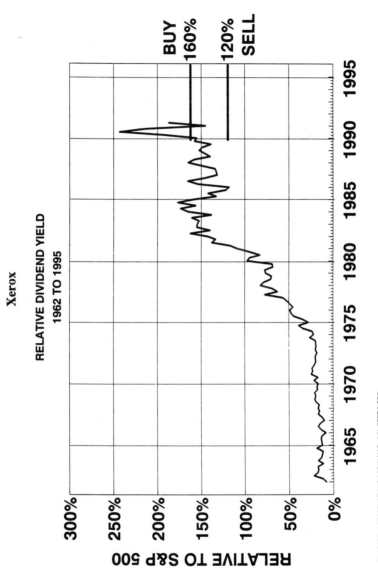

Xerox

RELATIVE DIVIDEND YIELD
1962 TO 1995

QUARTERLY OBSERVATIONS ARE IN MAR, JUN, SEPT & DEC

199

FIGURE C-26

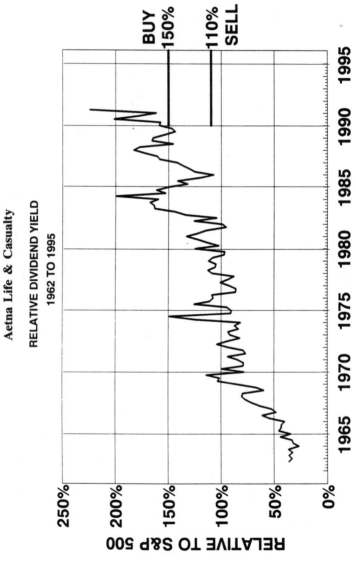

Aetna Life & Casualty

RELATIVE DIVIDEND YIELD
1962 TO 1995

QUARTERLY OBSERVATIONS ARE IN MAR, JUN, SEPT & DEC

200

FIGURE C-27

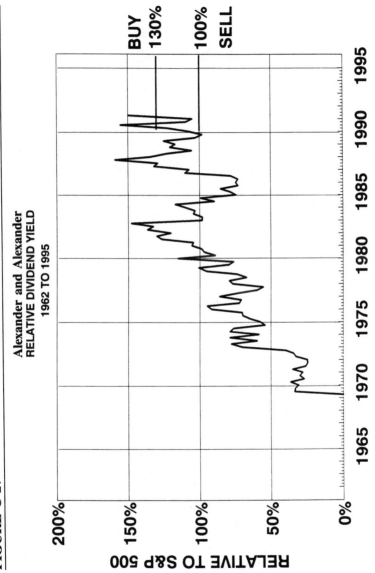

Alexander and Alexander
RELATIVE DIVIDEND YIELD
1962 TO 1995

QUARTERLY OBSERVATIONS ARE IN MAR, JUN, SEPT & DEC

FIGURE C-28

Allied Signal

RELATIVE DIVIDEND YIELD

1962 TO 1995

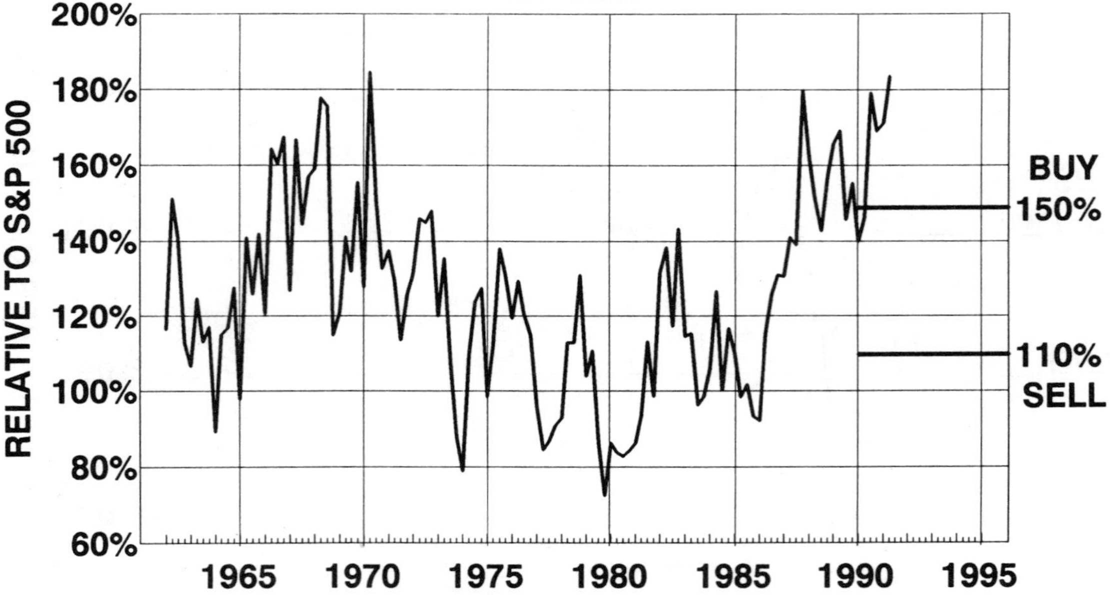

BUY
150%

110%
SELL

RELATIVE TO S&P 500

200%
180%
160%
140%
120%
100%
80%
60%

1965 1970 1975 1980 1985 1990 1995

QUARTERLY OBSERVATIONS ARE IN MAR, JUN, SEPT & DEC

202

FIGURE C-29

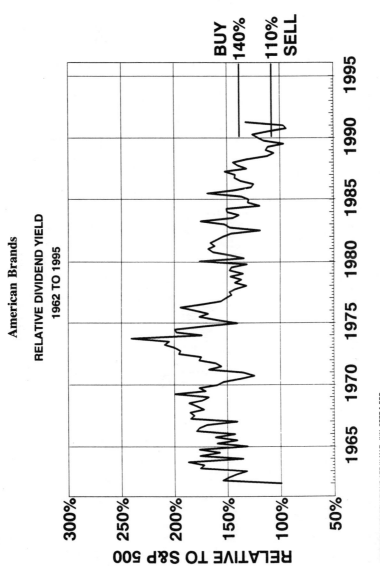

American Brands

RELATIVE DIVIDEND YIELD
1962 TO 1995

QUARTERLY OBSERVATIONS ARE IN MAR, JUN, SEPT & DEC

203

FIGURE C-30

American Telephone & Telegraph

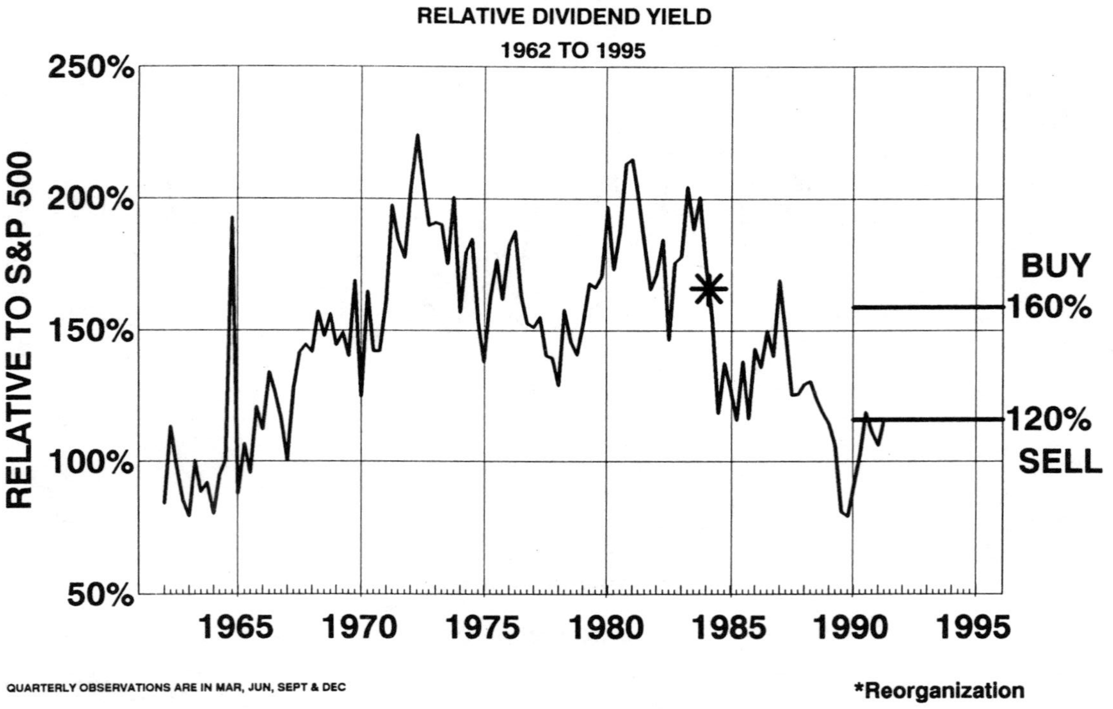
RELATIVE DIVIDEND YIELD
1962 TO 1995
250%
200%
150%
100%
50%
RELATIVE TO S&P 500
1965
1970
1975
1980
1985
1990
1995
BUY
160%
120%
SELL
QUARTERLY OBSERVATIONS ARE IN MAR, JUN, SEPT & DEC
*Reorganization

FIGURE C-31

Ameritech

RELATIVE DIVIDEND YIELD
1962 TO 1995

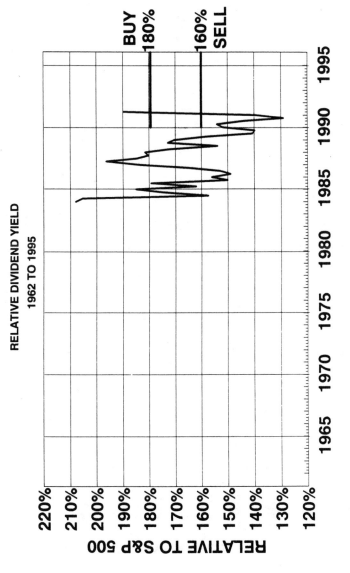

QUARTERLY OBSERVATIONS ARE IN MAR, JUN, SEPT & DEC

FIGURE C-32

Armstrong World

RELATIVE DIVIDEND YIELD
1962 TO 1995

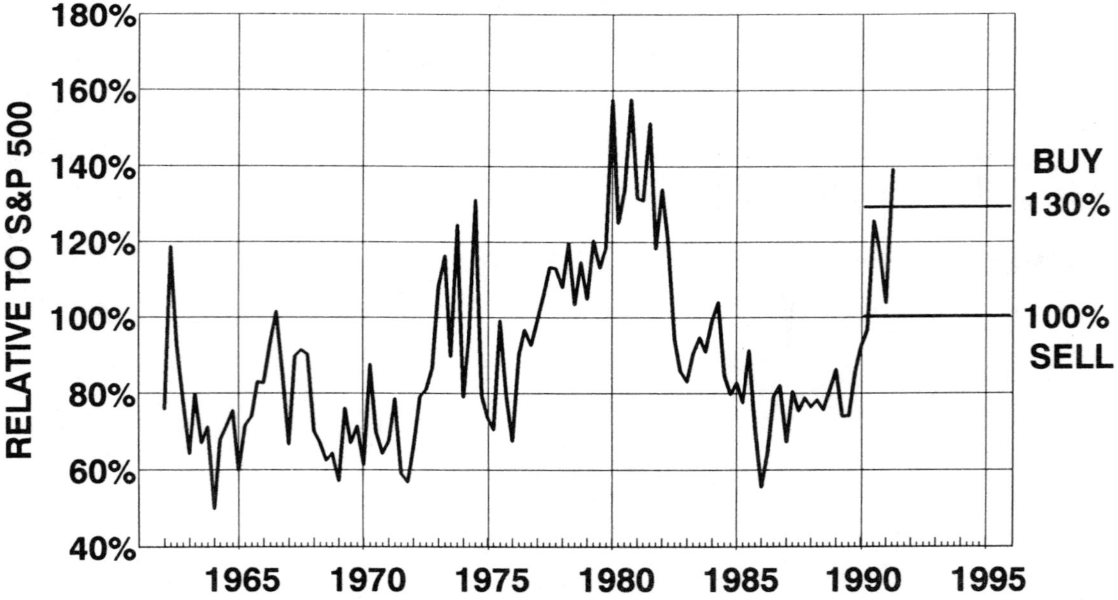

BUY
130%

100%
SELL

RELATIVE TO S&P 500

180%
160%
140%
120%
100%
80%
60%
40%

1965   1970   1975   1980   1985   1990   1995

QUARTERLY OBSERVATIONS ARE IN MAR, JUN, SEPT & DEC

206

FIGURE C-33

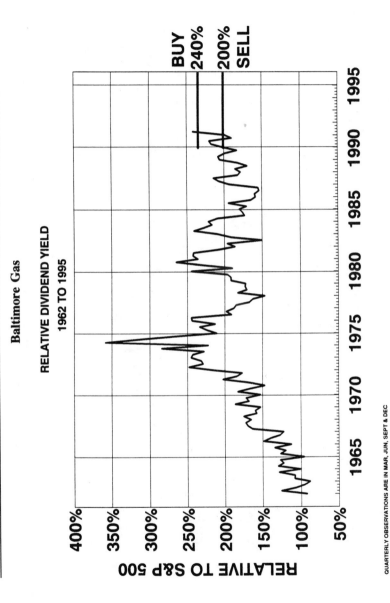

Baltimore Gas

RELATIVE DIVIDEND YIELD
1962 TO 1995

QUARTERLY OBSERVATIONS ARE IN MAR, JUN, SEPT & DEC

207

FIGURE C-34

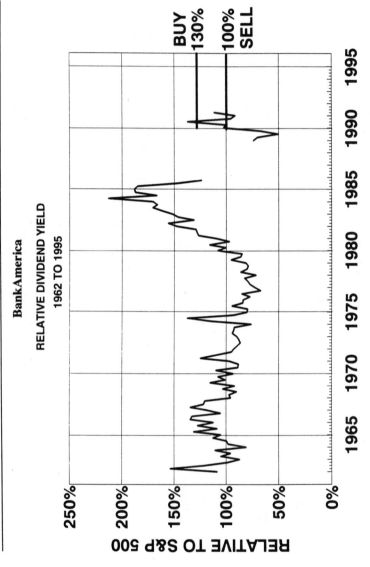

BankAmerica

RELATIVE DIVIDEND YIELD

1962 TO 1995

QUARTERLY OBSERVATIONS ARE IN MAR, JUN, SEPT & DEC

208

FIGURE C-35

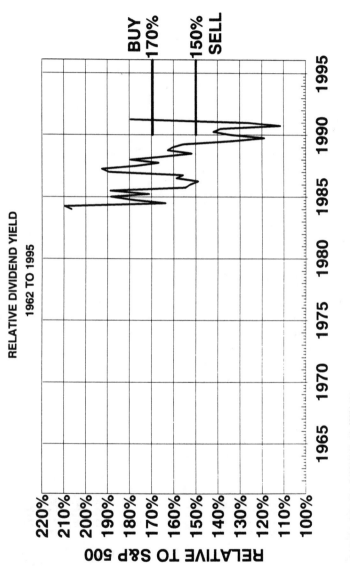

Bell Atlantic

RELATIVE DIVIDEND YIELD
1962 TO 1995

QUARTERLY OBSERVATIONS ARE IN MAR, JUN, SEPT & DEC

FIGURE C-36

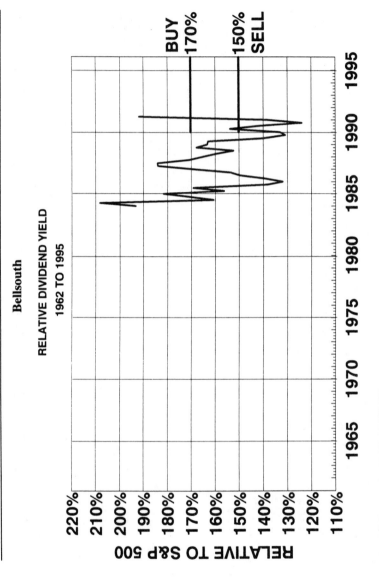

Bellsouth

RELATIVE DIVIDEND YIELD
1962 TO 1995

QUARTERLY OBSERVATIONS ARE IN MAR, JUN, SEPT & DEC

210

FIGURE C-37

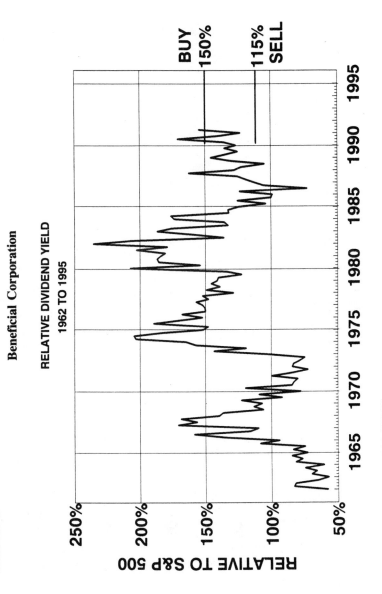

Beneficial Corporation

RELATIVE DIVIDEND YIELD
1962 TO 1995

QUARTERLY OBSERVATIONS ARE IN MAR, JUN, SEPT & DEC

211

FIGURE C-38

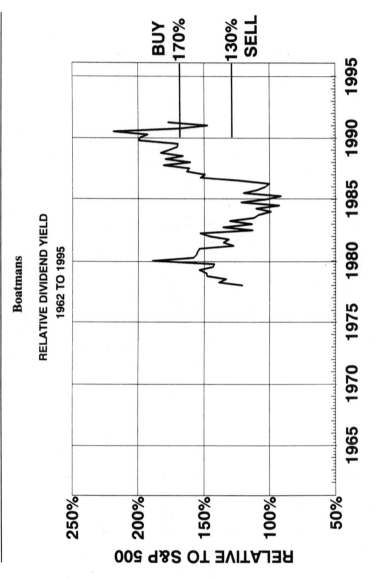

Boatmans

RELATIVE DIVIDEND YIELD
1962 TO 1995

BUY
170%

130%
SELL

QUARTERLY OBSERVATIONS ARE IN MAR, JUN, SEPT & DEC

212

FIGURE C-39

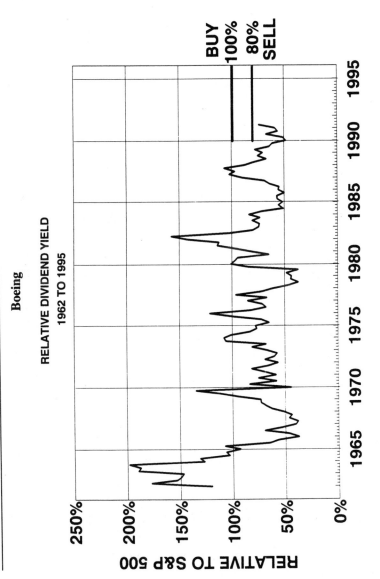

Boeing

RELATIVE DIVIDEND YIELD
1962 TO 1995

QUARTERLY OBSERVATIONS ARE IN MAR, JUN, SEPT & DEC

213

FIGURE C-40

Briggs & Stratton

RELATIVE DIVIDEND YIELD
1962 TO 1995

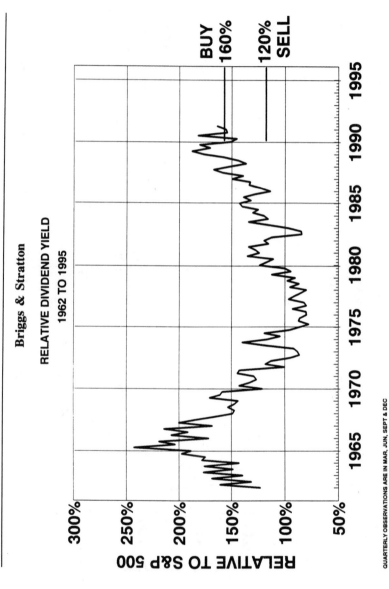

QUARTERLY OBSERVATIONS ARE IN MAR, JUN, SEPT & DEC

FIGURE C-41

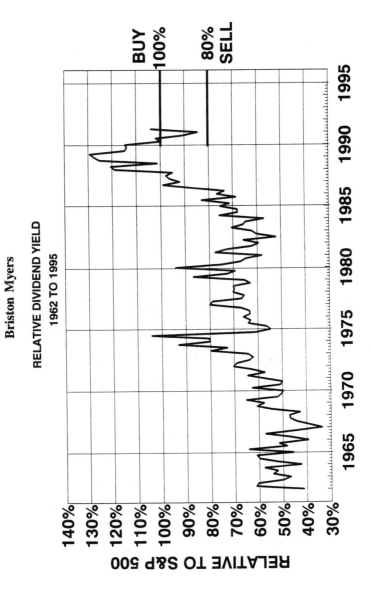

Briston Myers

RELATIVE DIVIDEND YIELD
1962 TO 1995

QUARTERLY OBSERVATIONS ARE IN MAR, JUN, SEPT & DEC

FIGURE C-42

Campbell Soup

RELATIVE DIVIDEND YIELD

1962 TO 1995

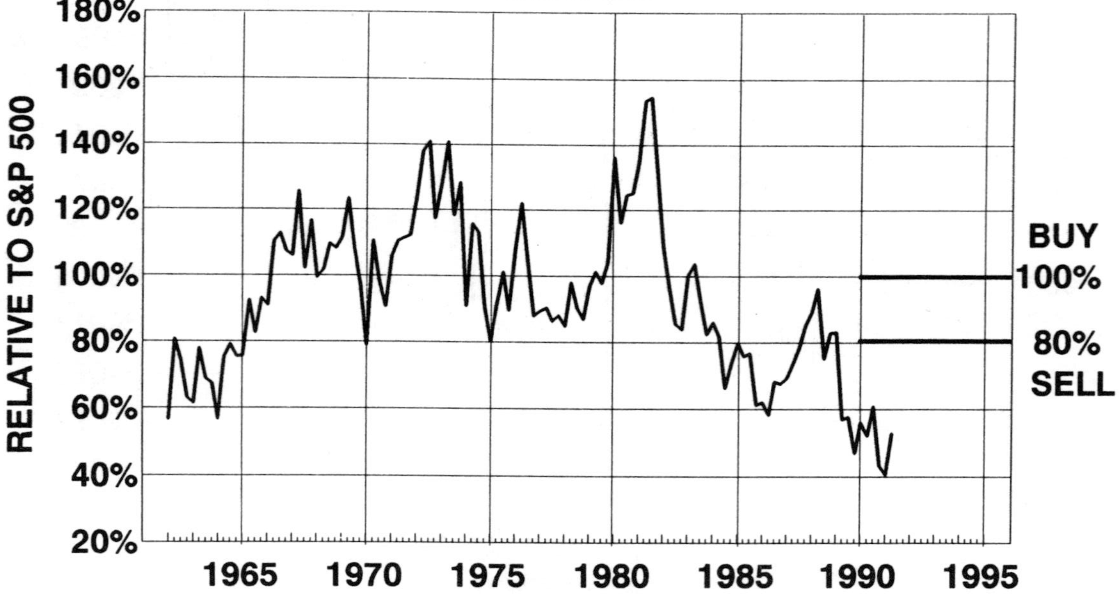

QUARTERLY OBSERVATIONS ARE IN MAR, JUN, SEPT & DEC

FIGURE C-43

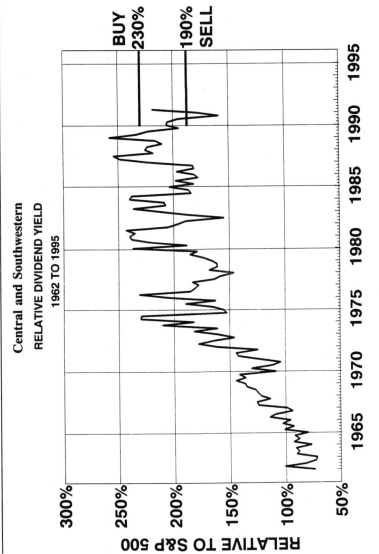

Central and Southwestern

RELATIVE DIVIDEND YIELD

1962 TO 1995

QUARTERLY OBSERVATIONS ARE IN MAR, JUN, SEPT & DEC

FIGURE C-44

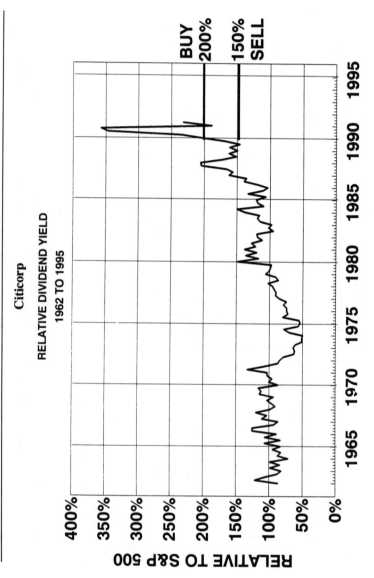

Citicorp

RELATIVE DIVIDEND YIELD
1962 TO 1995

QUARTERLY OBSERVATIONS ARE IN MAR, JUN, SEPT & DEC

218

FIGURE C-45

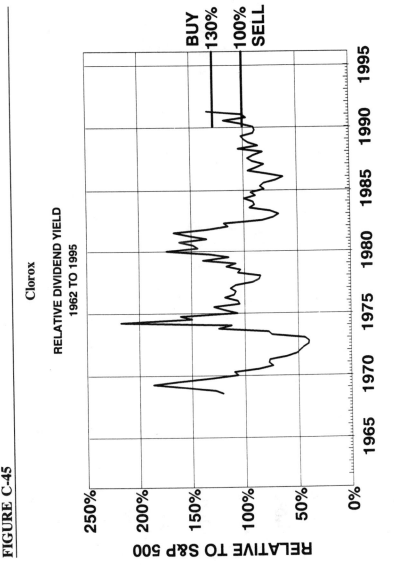

Clorox

RELATIVE DIVIDEND YIELD
1962 TO 1995

BUY
130%

100%
SELL

QUARTERLY OBSERVATIONS ARE IN MAR, JUN, SEPT & DEC

219

FIGURE C-46

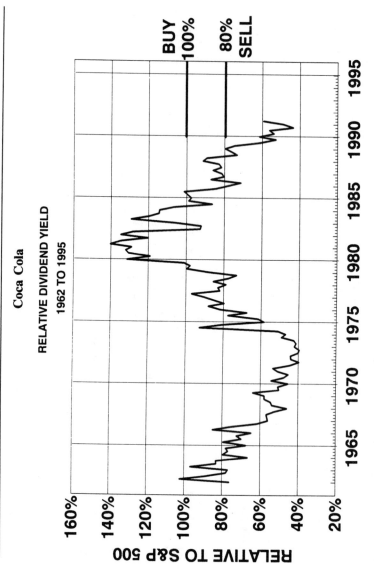

Coca Cola

RELATIVE DIVIDEND YIELD
1962 TO 1995

QUARTERLY OBSERVATIONS ARE IN MAR, JUN, SEPT & DEC

FIGURE C-47

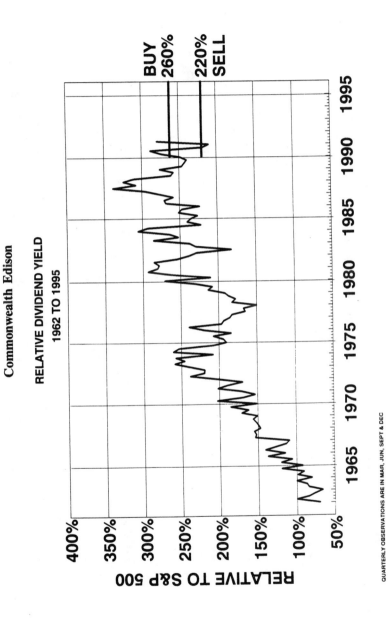

Commonwealth Edison

RELATIVE DIVIDEND YIELD
1962 TO 1995

QUARTERLY OBSERVATIONS ARE IN MAR, JUN, SEPT & DEC

FIGURE C-48

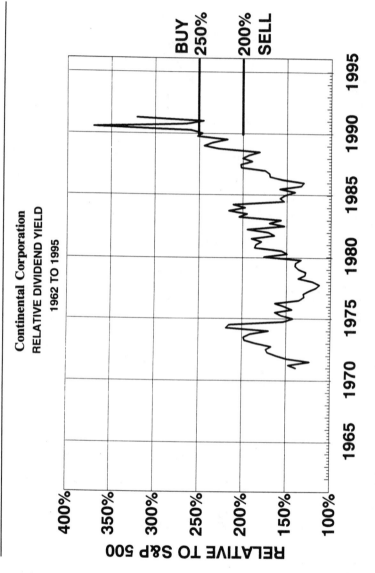

Continental Corporation
RELATIVE DIVIDEND YIELD
1962 TO 1995

BUY
250%

200%
SELL

RELATIVE TO S&P 500

400%
350%
300%
250%
200%
150%
100%

1965   1970   1975   1980   1985   1990   1995

QUARTERLY OBSERVATIONS ARE IN MAR, JUN, SEPT & DEC

FIGURE C-49

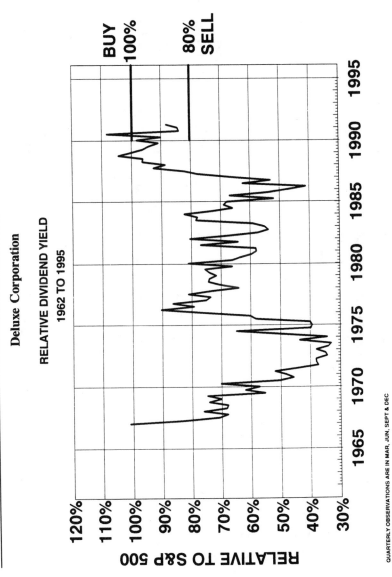

Deluxe Corporation

RELATIVE DIVIDEND YIELD
1962 TO 1995

QUARTERLY OBSERVATIONS ARE IN MAR, JUN, SEPT & DEC

FIGURE C-50

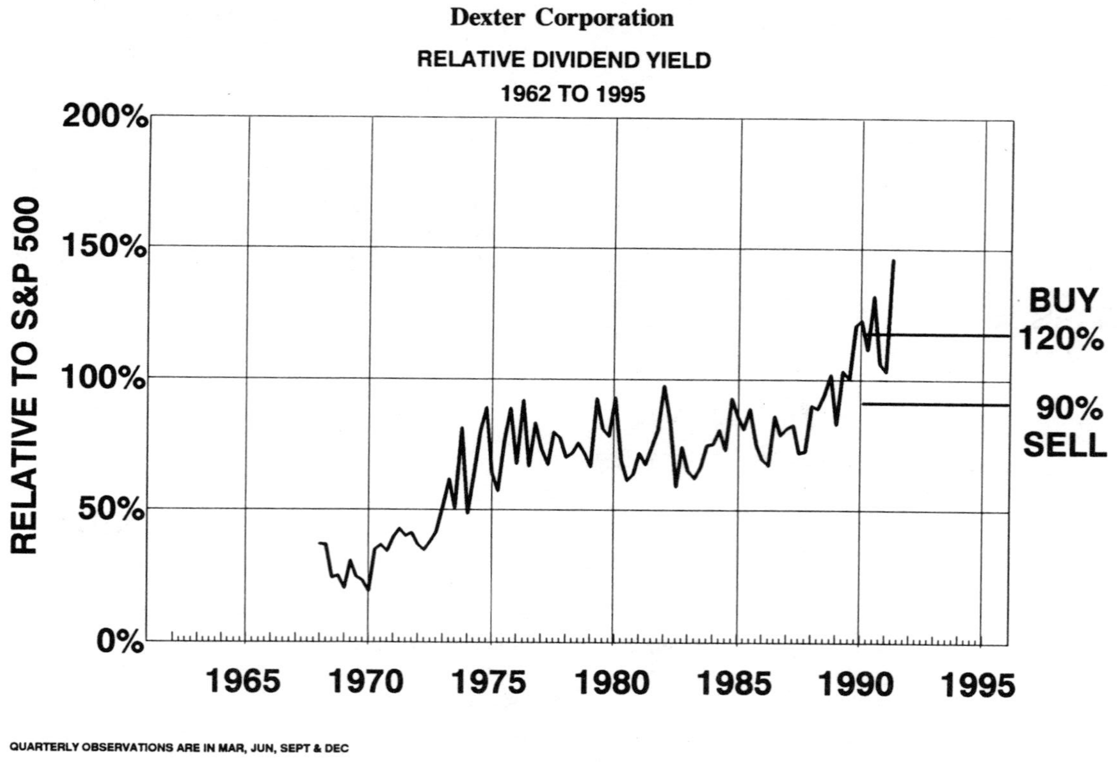
Dexter Corporation
RELATIVE DIVIDEND YIELD
1962 TO 1995
RELATIVE TO S&P 500
200%
150%
100%
50%
0%
1965
1970
1975
1980
1985
1990
1995
BUY
120%
90%
SELL
QUARTERLY OBSERVATIONS ARE IN MAR, JUN, SEPT & DEC

FIGURE C-51

Diebold

RELATIVE DIVIDEND YIELD
1962 TO 1995

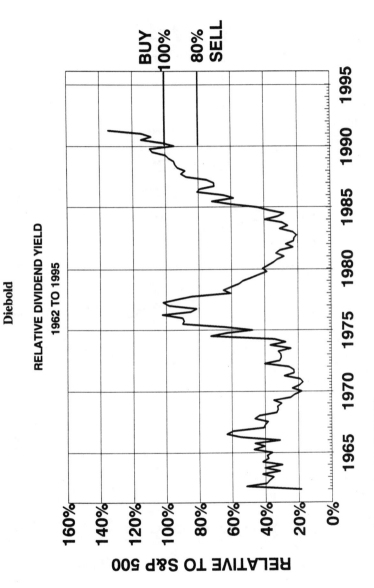

QUARTERLY OBSERVATIONS ARE IN MAR, JUN, SEPT & DEC

225

FIGURE C-52

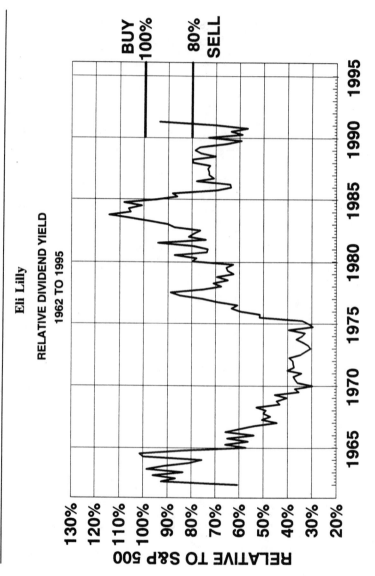

Eli Lilly

RELATIVE DIVIDEND YIELD
1962 TO 1995

QUARTERLY OBSERVATIONS ARE IN MAR, JUN, SEPT & DEC

FIGURE C-53

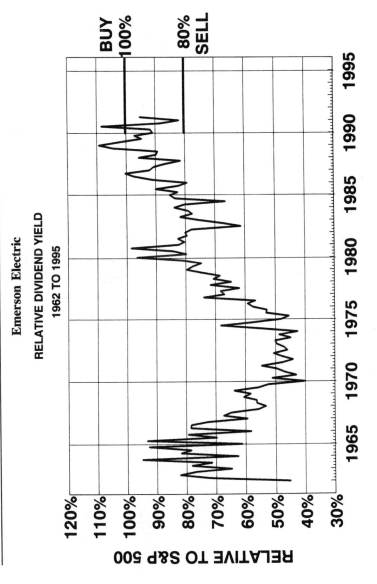

Emerson Electric

RELATIVE DIVIDEND YIELD

1962 TO 1995

QUARTERLY OBSERVATIONS ARE IN MAR, JUN, SEPT & DEC

FIGURE C-54

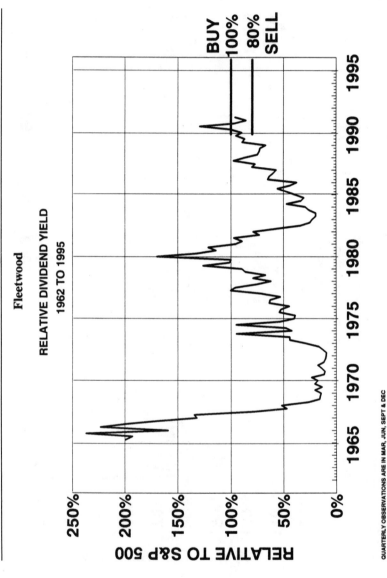

Fleetwood

RELATIVE DIVIDEND YIELD
1962 TO 1995

QUARTERLY OBSERVATIONS ARE IN MAR, JUN, SEPT & DEC

228

FIGURE C-55

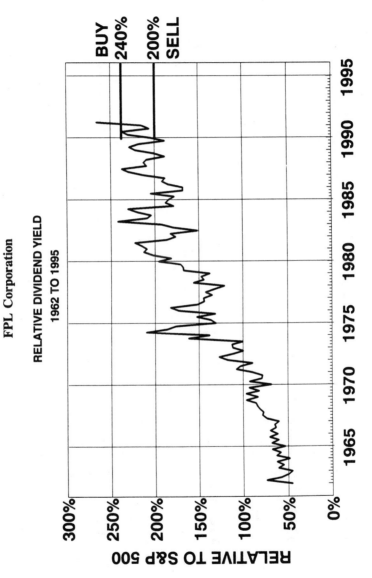

FPL Corporation

RELATIVE DIVIDEND YIELD
1962 TO 1995

BUY
240%

200%
SELL

300% 250% 200% 150% 100% 50% 0%

RELATIVE TO S&P 500

1965 1970 1975 1980 1985 1990 1995

QUARTERLY OBSERVATIONS ARE IN MAR, JUN, SEPT & DEC

FIGURE C-56

General Electric

RELATIVE DIVIDEND YIELD
1962 TO 1995

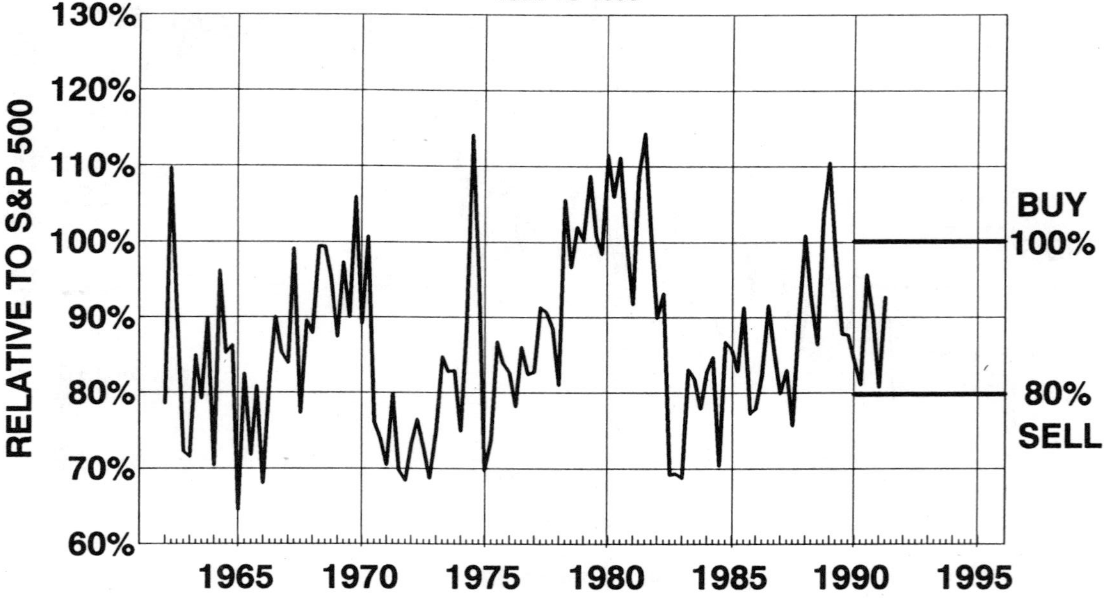

QUARTERLY OBSERVATIONS ARE IN MAR, JUN, SEPT & DEC

230

FIGURE C-57

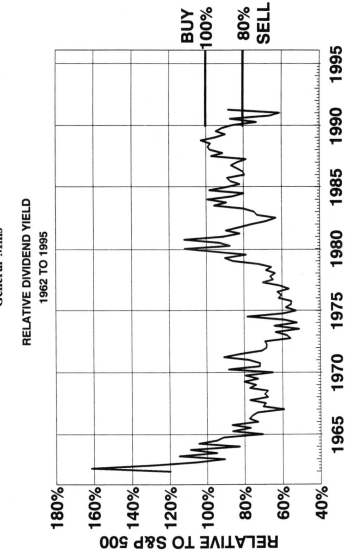

General Mills

RELATIVE DIVIDEND YIELD
1962 TO 1995

QUARTERLY OBSERVATIONS ARE IN MAR, JUN, SEPT & DEC

FIGURE C-58

General Signal

RELATIVE DIVIDEND YIELD
1962 TO 1995

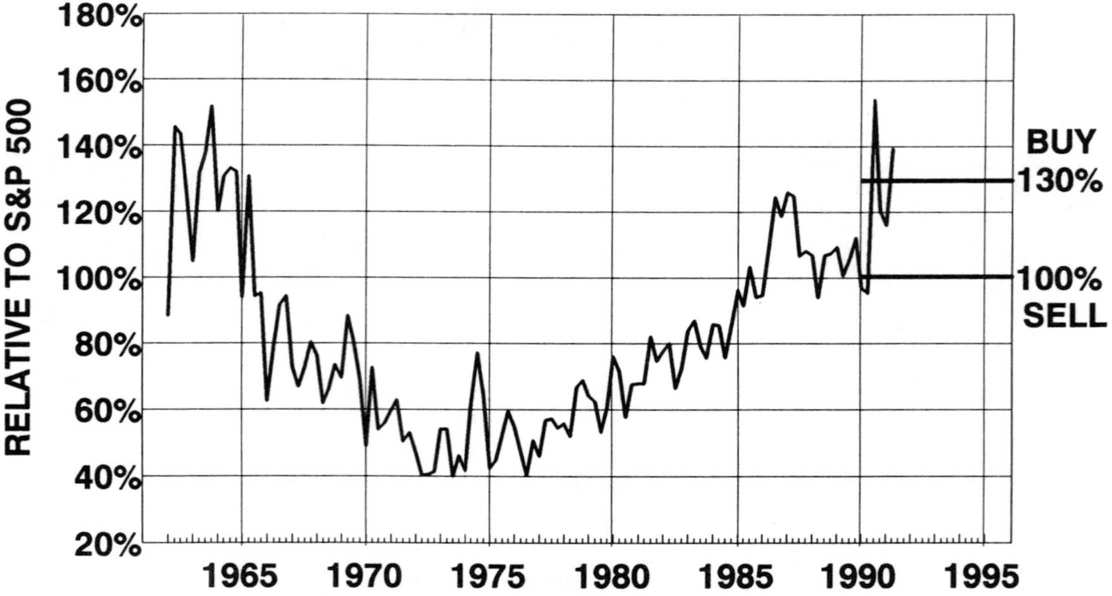

QUARTERLY OBSERVATIONS ARE IN MAR, JUN, SEPT & DEC

232

FIGURE C-59

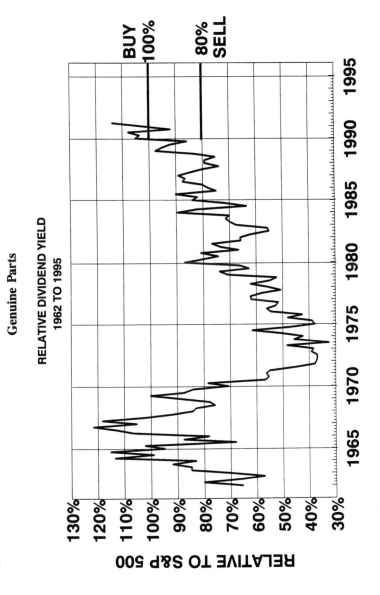

Genuine Parts

RELATIVE DIVIDEND YIELD
1962 TO 1995

QUARTERLY OBSERVATIONS ARE IN MAR, JUN, SEPT & DEC

FIGURE C-60

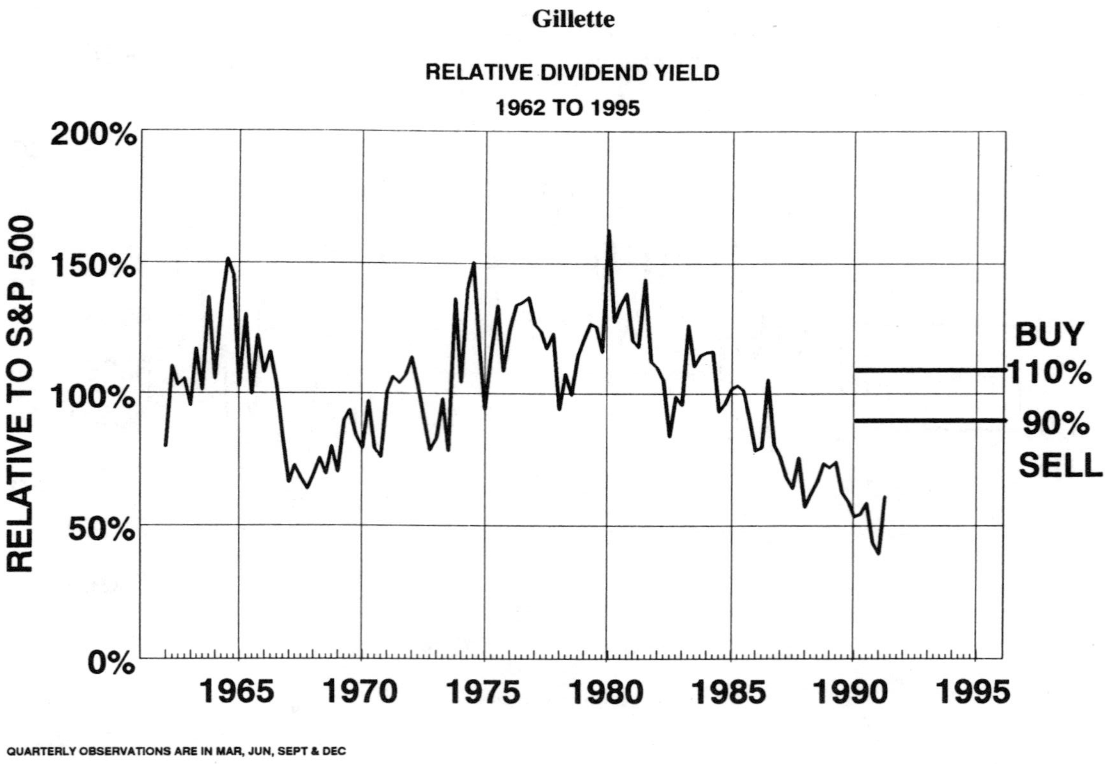

Gillette

RELATIVE DIVIDEND YIELD

1962 TO 1995

QUARTERLY OBSERVATIONS ARE IN MAR, JUN, SEPT & DEC

234

FIGURE C-61

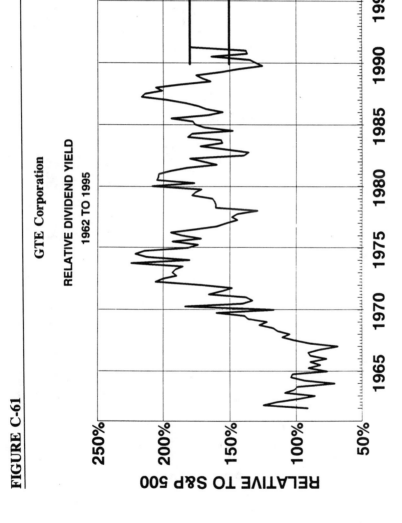

GTE Corporation

RELATIVE DIVIDEND YIELD
1962 TO 1995

QUARTERLY OBSERVATIONS ARE IN MAR, JUN, SEPT & DEC

FIGURE C-62

Halliburton

RELATIVE DIVIDEND YIELD

1962 TO 1995

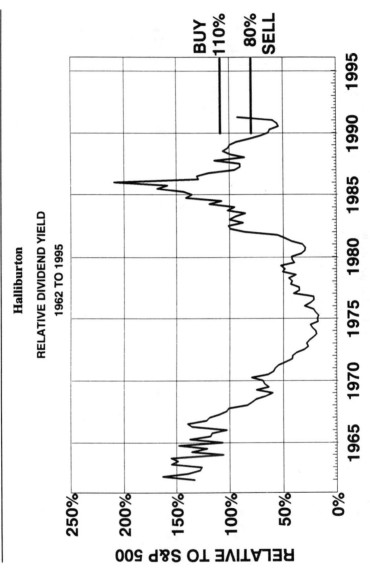

QUARTERLY OBSERVATIONS ARE IN MAR, JUN, SEPT & DEC

FIGURE C-63

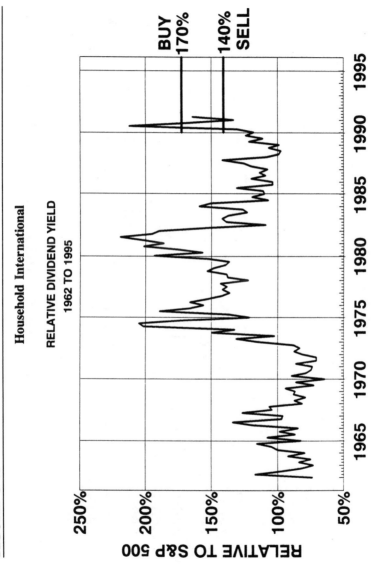

Household International

RELATIVE DIVIDEND YIELD
1962 TO 1995

BUY
170%

140%
SELL

QUARTERLY OBSERVATIONS ARE IN MAR, JUN, SEPT & DEC

FIGURE C-64

International Paper

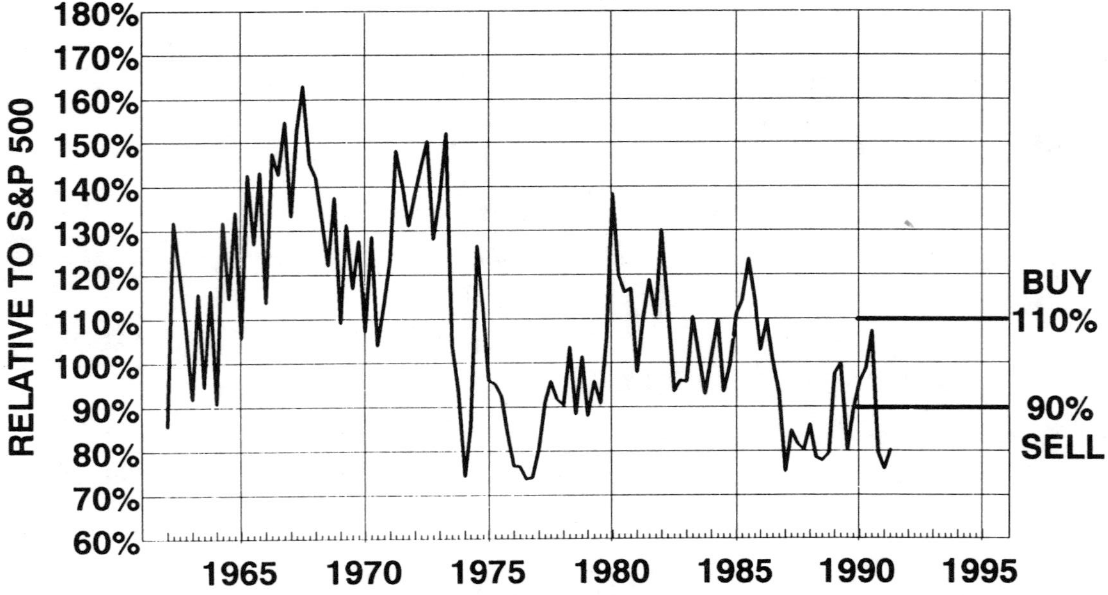
RELATIVE DIVIDEND YIELD
1962 TO 1995
RELATIVE TO S&P 500
180%
170%
160%
150%
140%
130%
120%
110%
100%
90%
80%
70%
60%
1965
1970
1975
1980
1985
1990
1995
BUY
110%
90%
SELL
QUARTERLY OBSERVATIONS ARE IN MAR, JUN, SEPT & DEC

FIGURE C-65

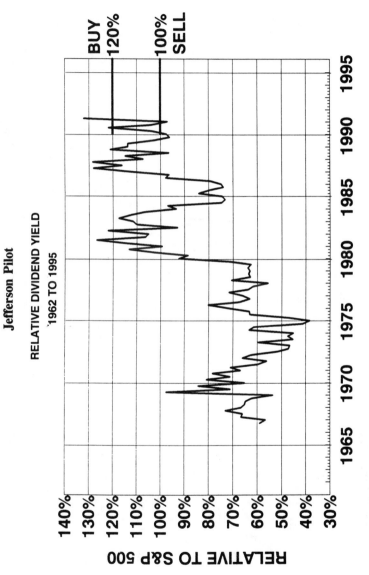

Jefferson Pilot

RELATIVE DIVIDEND YIELD
1962 TO 1995

QUARTERLY OBSERVATIONS ARE IN MAR, JUN, SEPT & DEC

239

FIGURE C-66

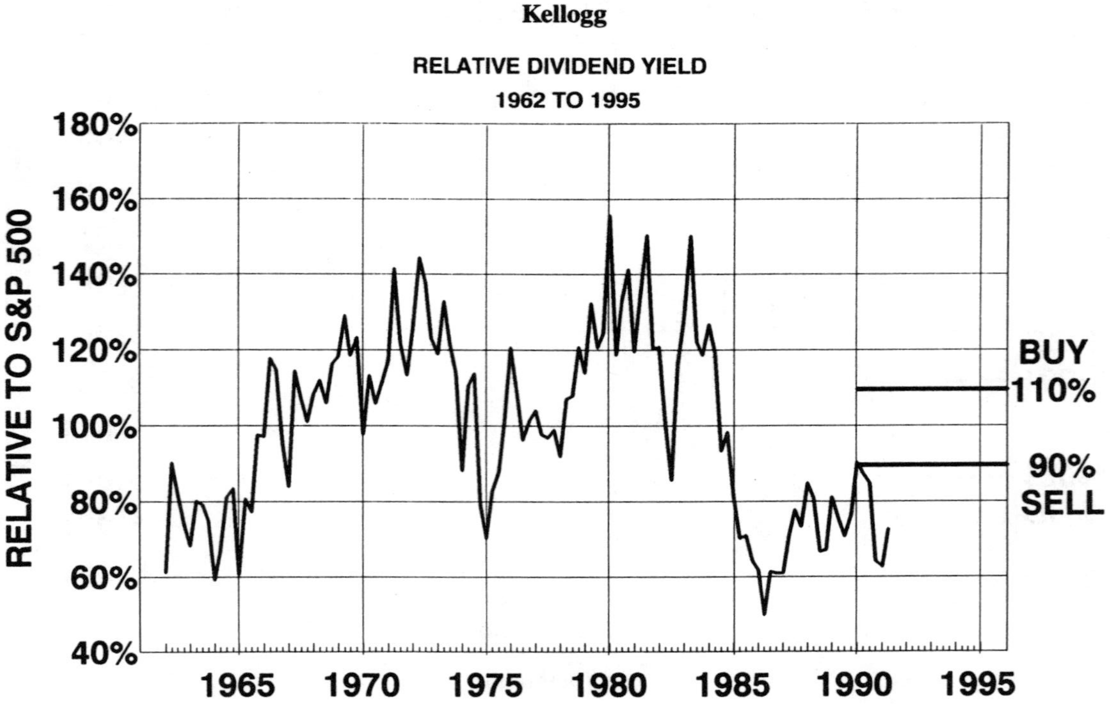

Kellogg

RELATIVE DIVIDEND YIELD
1962 TO 1995

QUARTERLY OBSERVATIONS ARE IN MAR, JUN, SEPT & DEC

FIGURE C-67

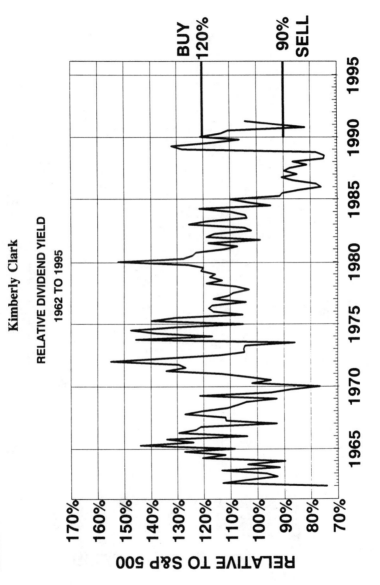

Kimberly Clark

RELATIVE DIVIDEND YIELD
1962 TO 1995

QUARTERLY OBSERVATIONS ARE IN MAR, JUN, SEPT & DEC

241

FIGURE C-68

McGraw-Hill

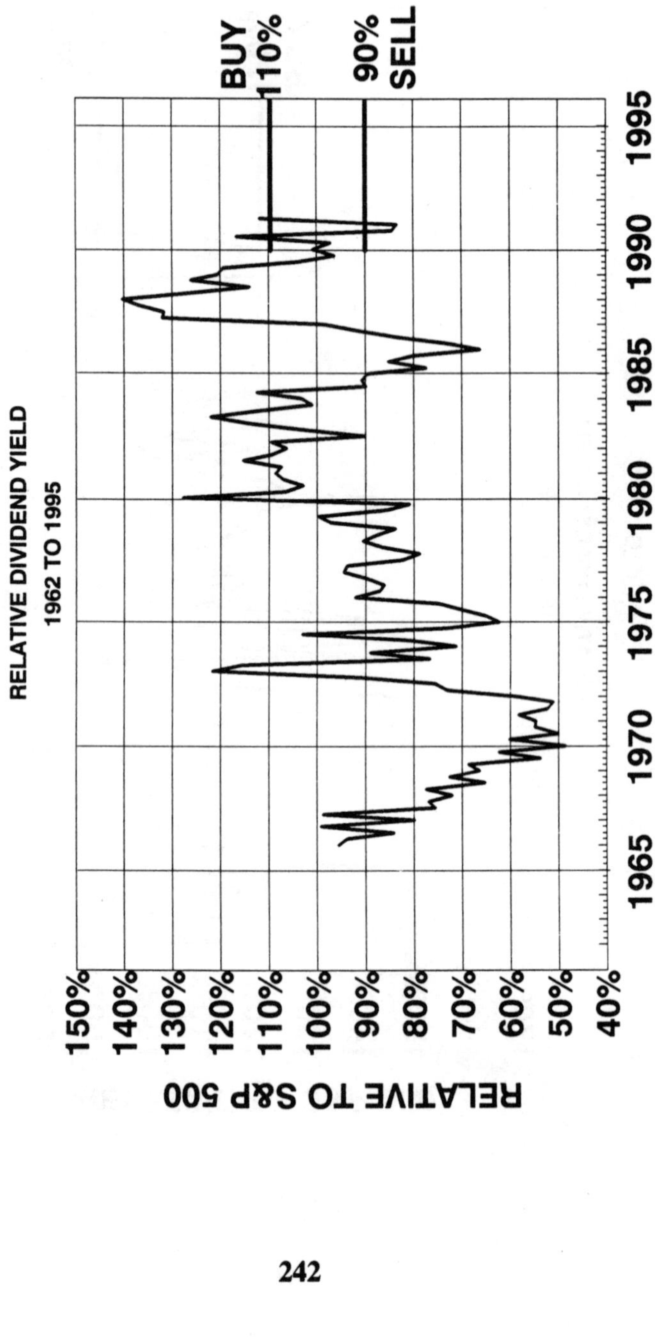

RELATIVE DIVIDEND YIELD
1962 TO 1995

BUY
110%

90%
SELL

RELATIVE TO S&P 500

150%
140%
130%
120%
110%
100%
90%
80%
70%
60%
50%
40%

1965 1970 1975 1980 1985 1990 1995

QUARTERLY OBSERVATIONS ARE IN MAR, JUN, SEPT & DEC

FIGURE C-69

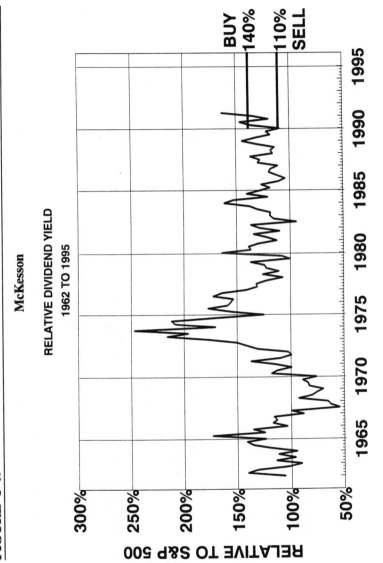

McKesson

RELATIVE DIVIDEND YIELD
1962 TO 1995

QUARTERLY OBSERVATIONS ARE IN MAR, JUN, SEPT & DEC

243

FIGURE C-70

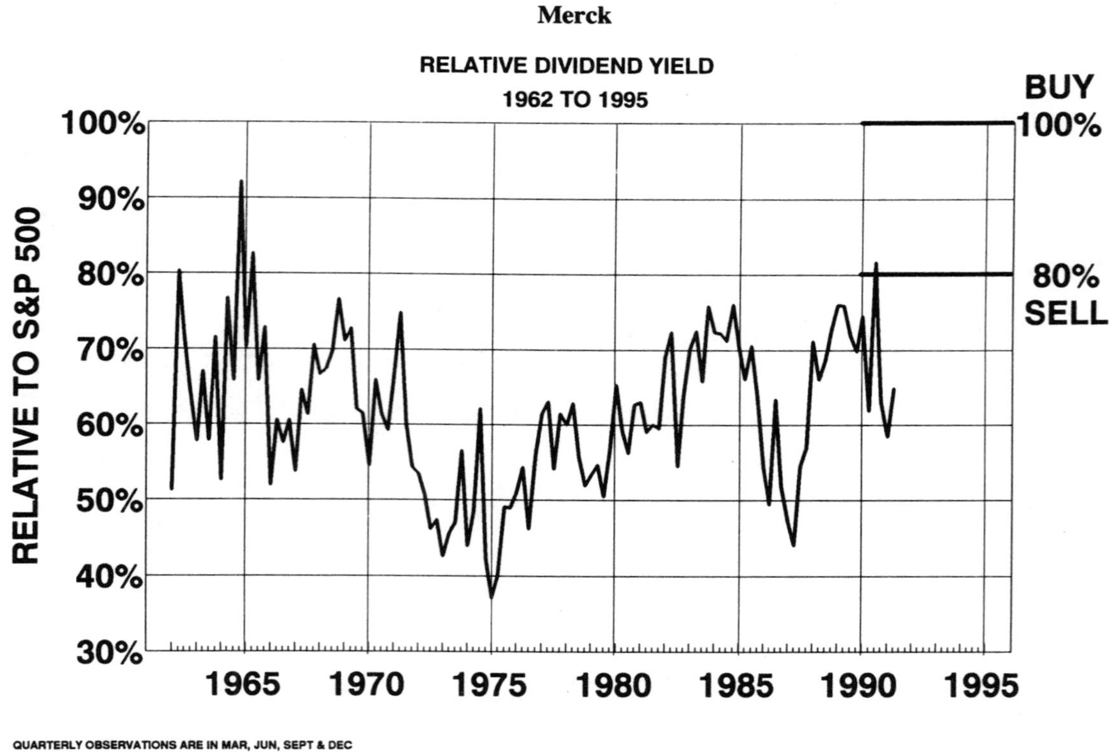

Merck

RELATIVE DIVIDEND YIELD
1962 TO 1995

QUARTERLY OBSERVATIONS ARE IN MAR, JUN, SEPT & DEC

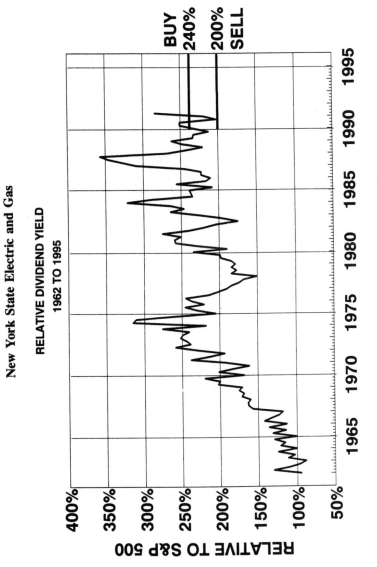

FIGURE C-71

New York State Electric and Gas

RELATIVE DIVIDEND YIELD
1962 TO 1995

QUARTERLY OBSERVATIONS ARE IN MAR, JUN, SEPT & DEC

245

FIGURE C-72

Northeast Utilities

RELATIVE DIVIDEND YIELD

1962 TO 1995

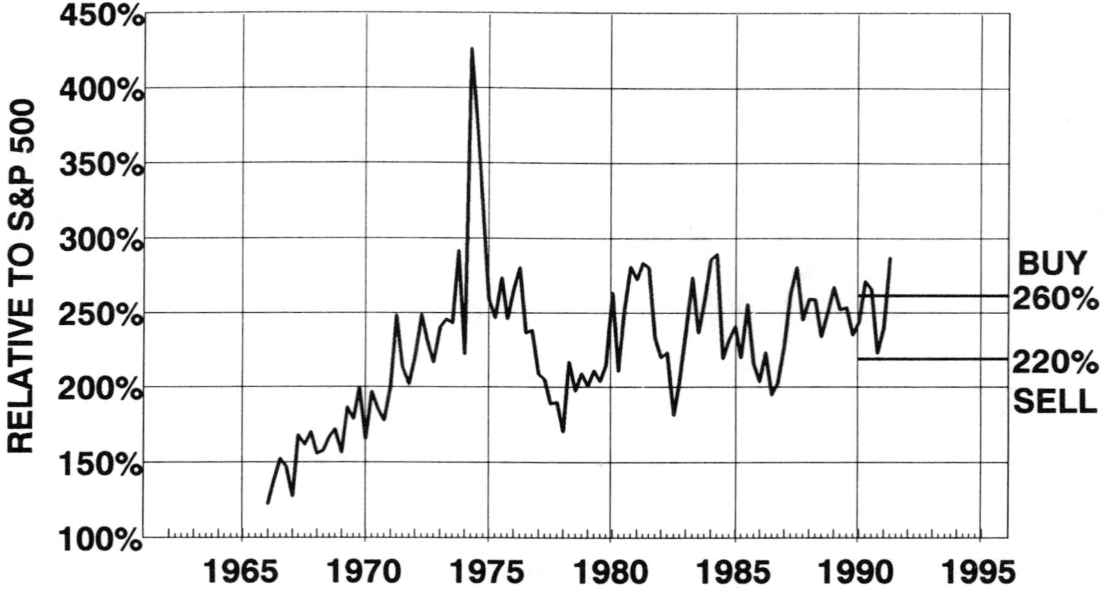

QUARTERLY OBSERVATIONS ARE IN MAR, JUN, SEPT & DEC

246

FIGURE C-73

Oklahoma Gas and Electric

RELATIVE DIVIDEND YIELD
1962 TO 1995

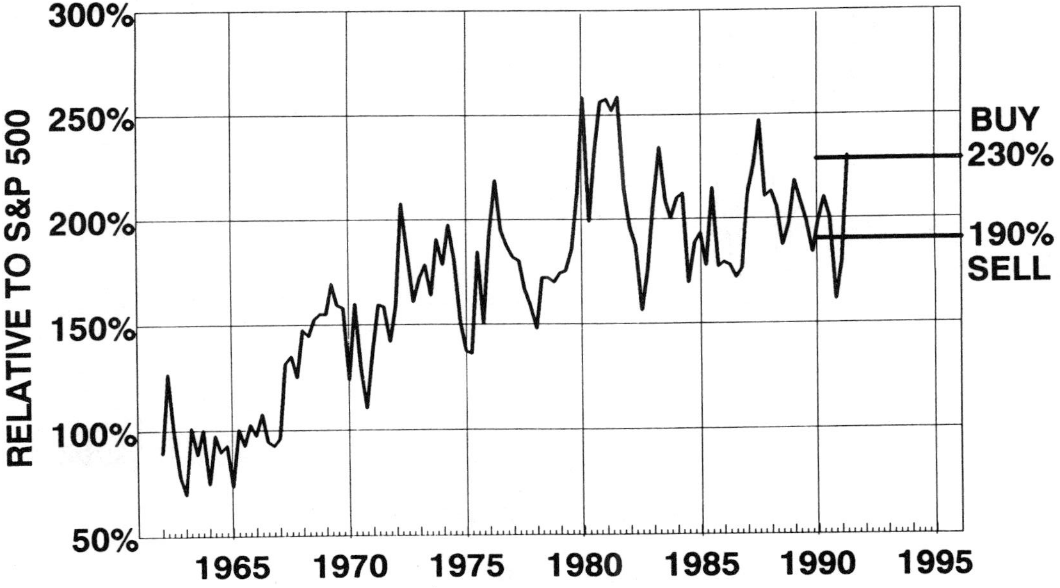

QUARTERLY OBSERVATIONS ARE IN MAR, JUN, SEPT & DEC

247

FIGURE C-74

Pacific Telesis

RELATIVE DIVIDEND YIELD
1962 TO 1995

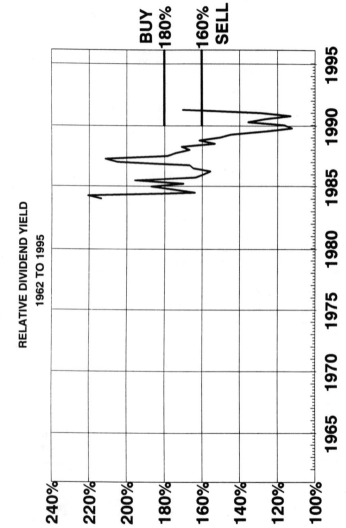

QUARTERLY OBSERVATIONS ARE IN MAR, JUN, SEPT & DEC

248

FIGURE C-75

Pennsylvania Power

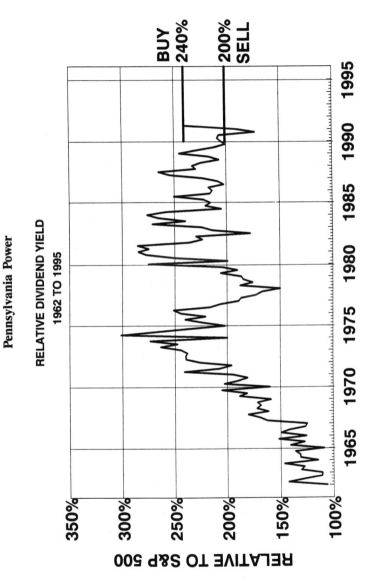

RELATIVE DIVIDEND YIELD
1962 TO 1995

QUARTERLY OBSERVATIONS ARE IN MAR, JUN, SEPT & DEC

249

FIGURE C-76

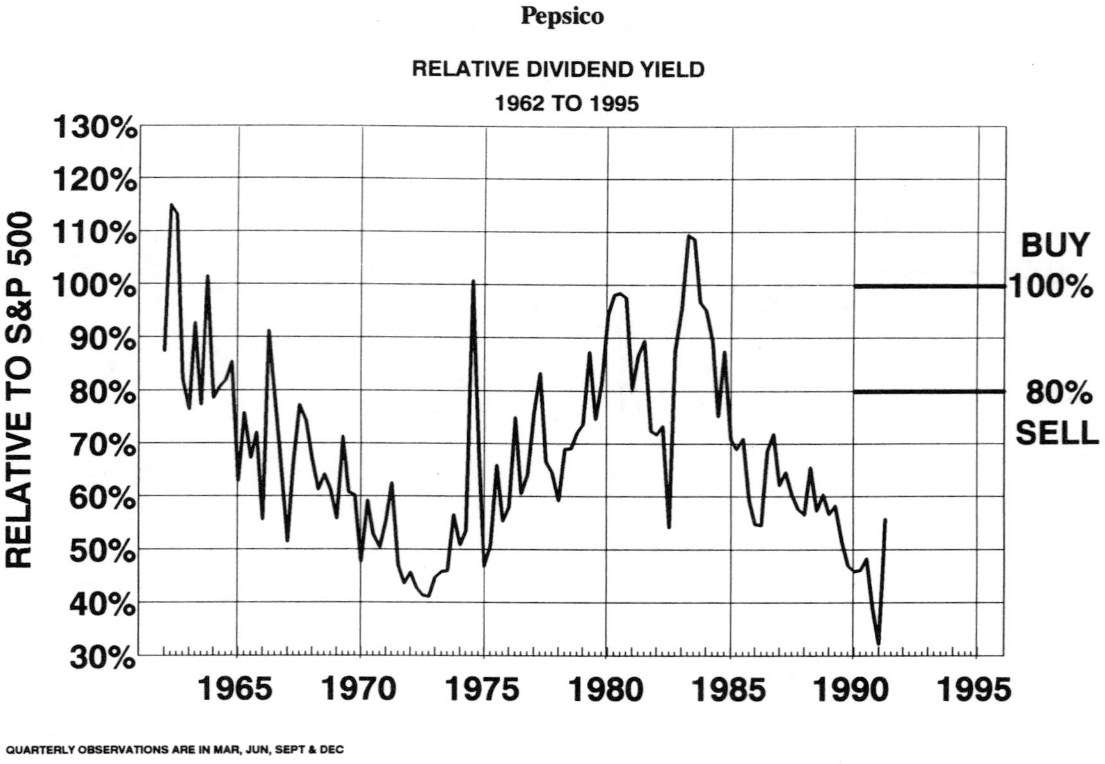

Pepsico

RELATIVE DIVIDEND YIELD

1962 TO 1995

QUARTERLY OBSERVATIONS ARE IN MAR, JUN, SEPT & DEC

FIGURE C-77

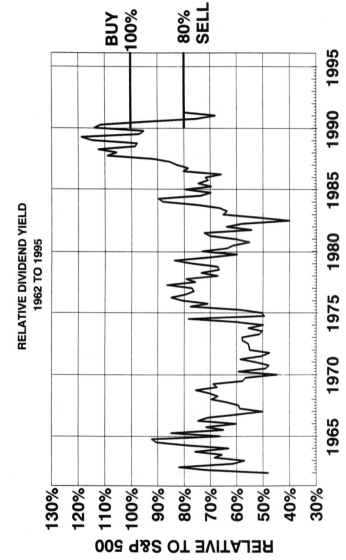

Pfizer

RELATIVE DIVIDEND YIELD
1962 TO 1995

251

FIGURE C-78

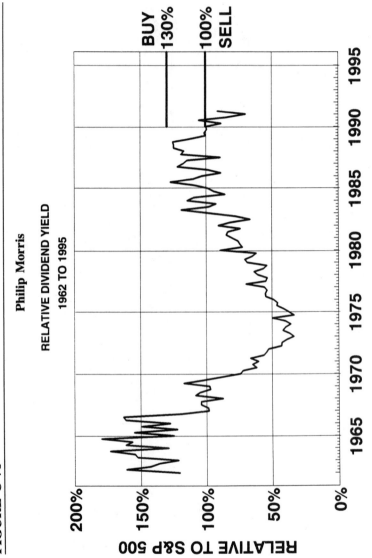

Philip Morris

RELATIVE DIVIDEND YIELD

1962 TO 1995

QUARTERLY OBSERVATIONS ARE IN MAR, JUN, SEPT & DEC

FIGURE C-79

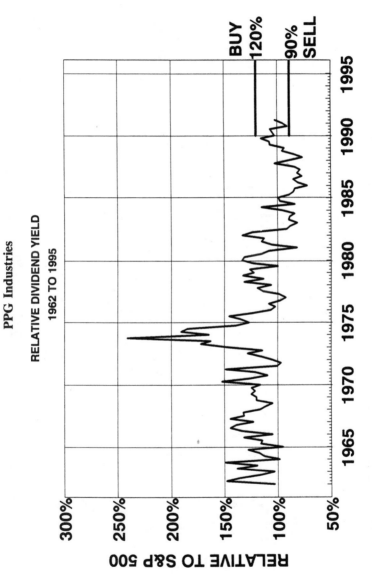

PPG Industries

RELATIVE DIVIDEND YIELD
1962 TO 1995

QUARTERLY OBSERVATIONS ARE IN MAR, JUN, SEPT & DEC

253

FIGURE C-80

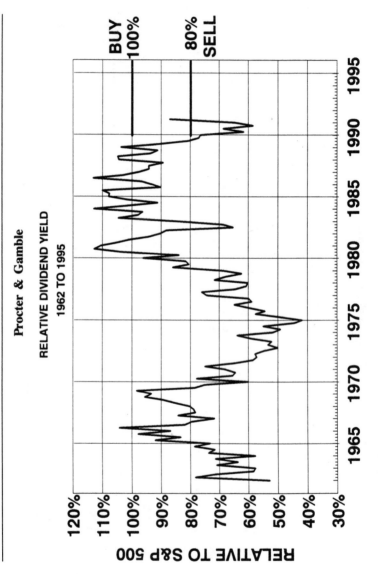

Procter & Gamble

RELATIVE DIVIDEND YIELD
1962 TO 1995

QUARTERLY OBSERVATIONS ARE IN MAR, JUN, SEPT & DEC

254

FIGURE C-81

Public Service Enterprise Group

RELATIVE DIVIDEND YIELD
1962 TO 1995

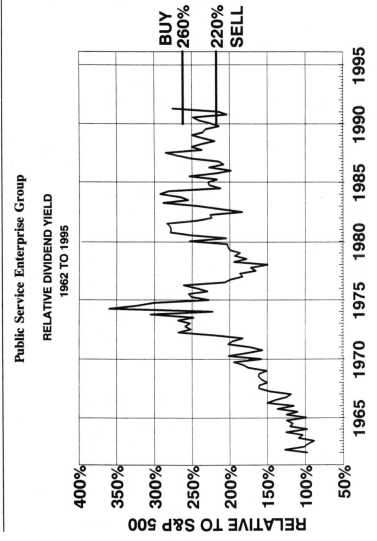

QUARTERLY OBSERVATIONS ARE IN MAR, JUN, SEPT & DEC

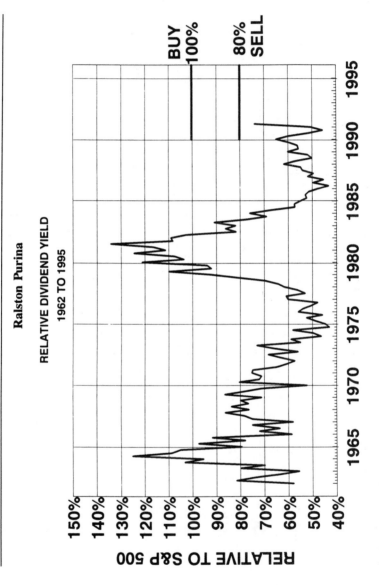

FIGURE C-82

Ralston Purina

RELATIVE DIVIDEND YIELD
1962 TO 1995

QUARTERLY OBSERVATIONS ARE IN MAR, JUN, SEPT & DEC

256

FIGURE C-83

Snap-On Tools

RELATIVE DIVIDEND YIELD
1962 TO 1995

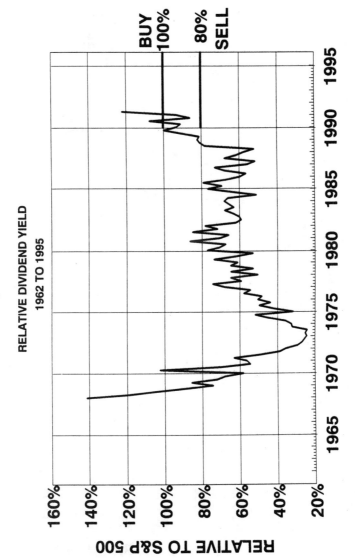

BUY
100%

80%
SELL

RELATIVE TO S&P 500

160%
140%
120%
100%
80%
60%
40%
20%

1965   1970   1975   1980   1985   1990   1995

QUARTERLY OBSERVATIONS ARE IN MAR, JUN, SEPT & DEC

257

FIGURE C-84

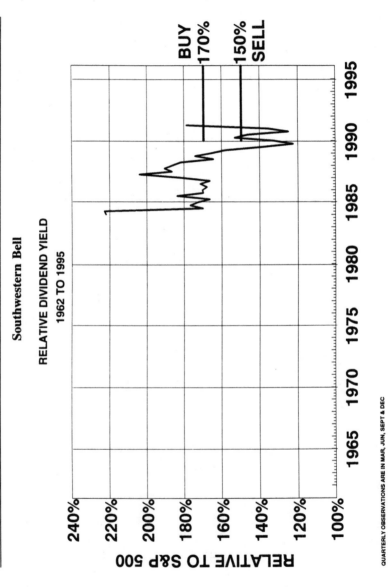

Southwestern Bell

RELATIVE DIVIDEND YIELD
1962 TO 1995

RELATIVE TO S&P 500

BUY
170%

150%
SELL

QUARTERLY OBSERVATIONS ARE IN MAR, JUN, SEPT & DEC

258

FIGURE C-85

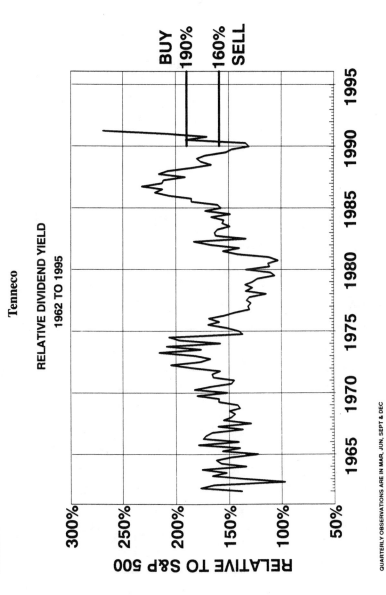

Tenneco

RELATIVE DIVIDEND YIELD
1962 TO 1995

QUARTERLY OBSERVATIONS ARE IN MAR, JUN, SEPT & DEC

FIGURE C-86

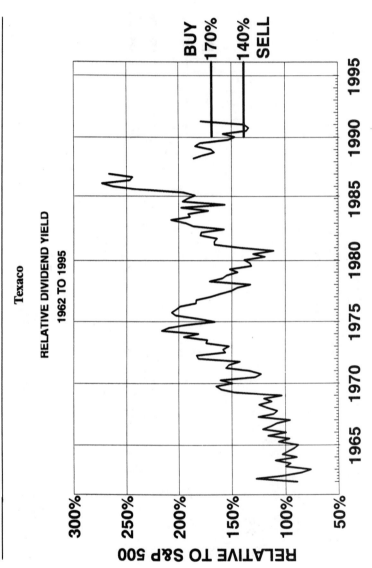

Texaco

RELATIVE DIVIDEND YIELD
1962 TO 1995

RELATIVE TO S&P 500

BUY
170%
140%
SELL

QUARTERLY OBSERVATIONS ARE IN MAR, JUN, SEPT & DEC

FIGURE C-87

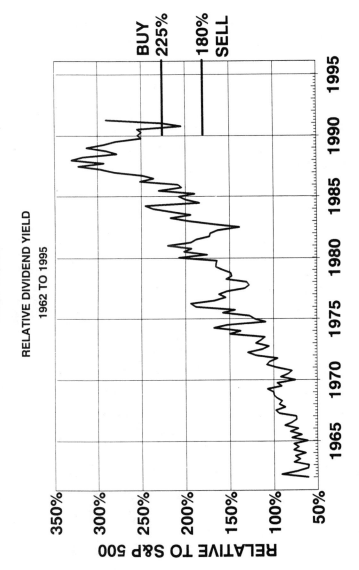

Texas Utilities

RELATIVE DIVIDEND YIELD
1962 TO 1995

QUARTERLY OBSERVATIONS ARE IN MAR, JUN, SEPT & DEC

261

FIGURE C-88

Thomas & Betts

RELATIVE DIVIDEND YIELD
1962 TO 1995

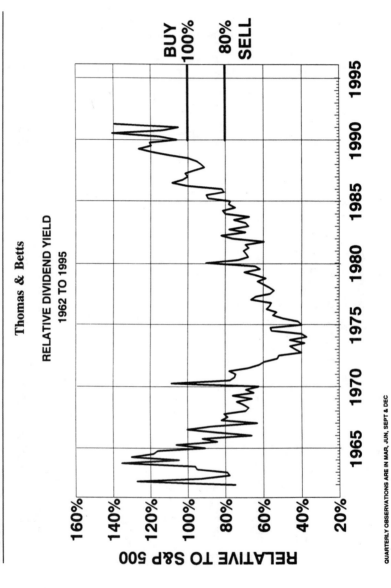

QUARTERLY OBSERVATIONS ARE IN MAR, JUN, SEPT & DEC

FIGURE C-89

Times Mirror

RELATIVE DIVIDEND YIELD
1962 TO 1995

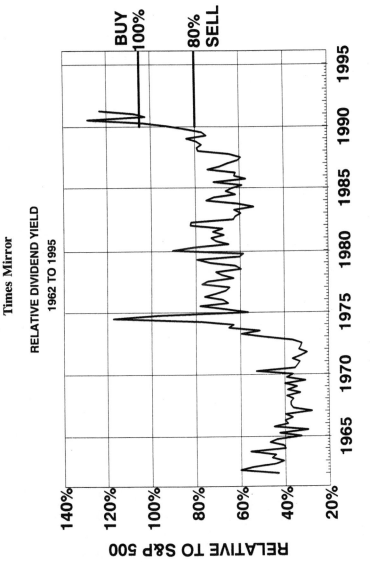

QUARTERLY OBSERVATIONS ARE IN MAR, JUN, SEPT & DEC

263

FIGURE C-90

U.S. West

RELATIVE DIVIDEND YIELD
1962 TO 1995

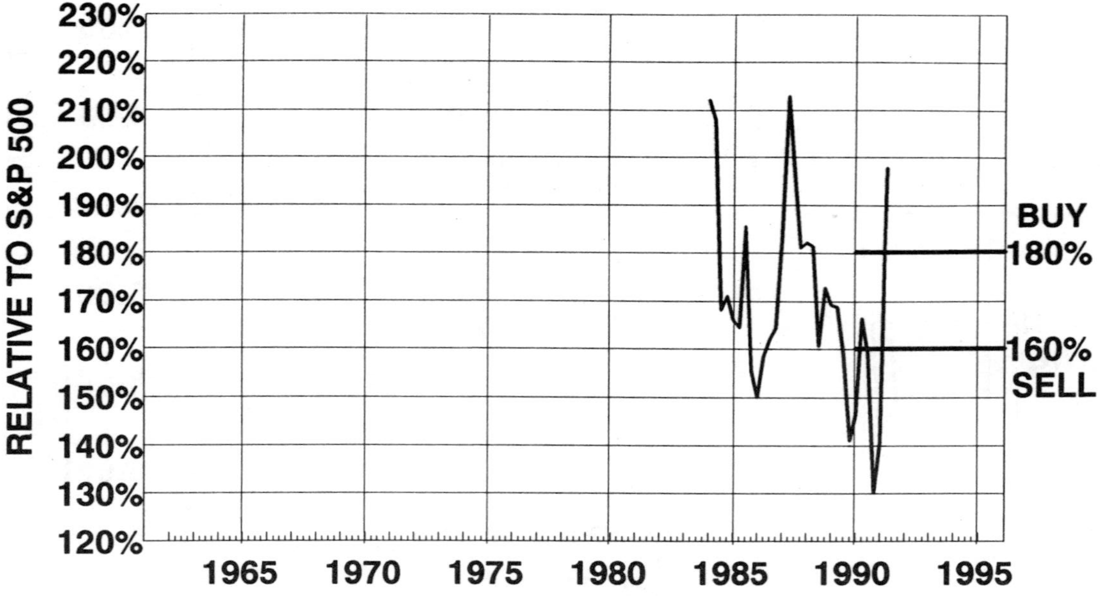

QUARTERLY OBSERVATIONS ARE IN MAR, JUN, SEPT & DEC

264

FIGURE C-91

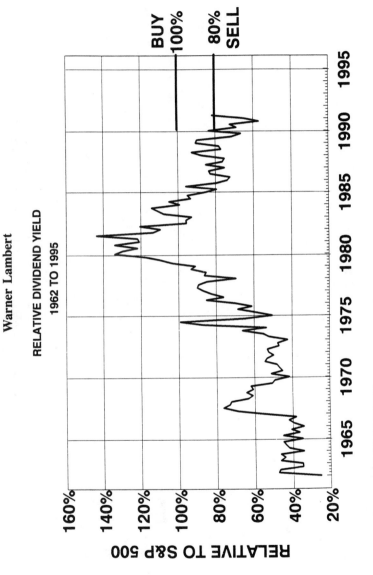

Warner Lambert

RELATIVE DIVIDEND YIELD
1962 TO 1995

QUARTERLY OBSERVATIONS ARE IN MAR, JUN, SEPT & DEC

265

FIGURE C-92

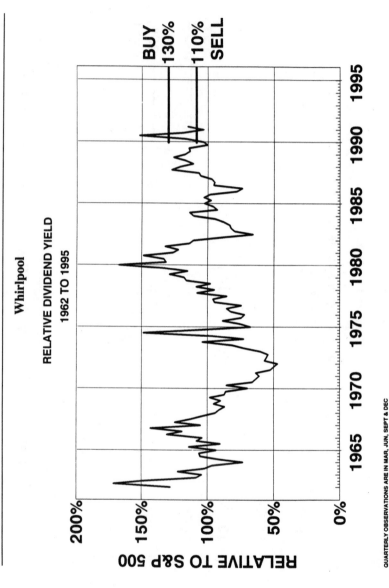

Whirlpool

RELATIVE DIVIDEND YIELD
1962 TO 1995

QUARTERLY OBSERVATIONS ARE IN MAR, JUN, SEPT & DEC

FIGURE C-93

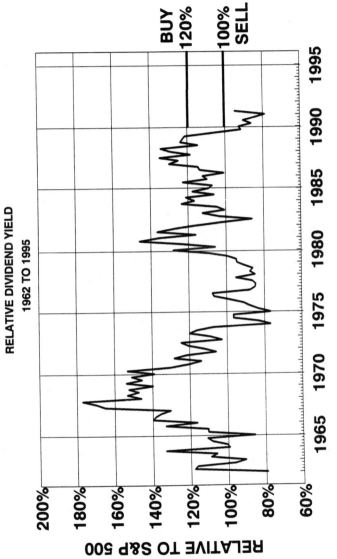

Winn Dixie Stores

RELATIVE DIVIDEND YIELD
1962 TO 1995

QUARTERLY OBSERVATIONS ARE IN MAR, JUN, SEPT & DEC

267

FIGURE C-94

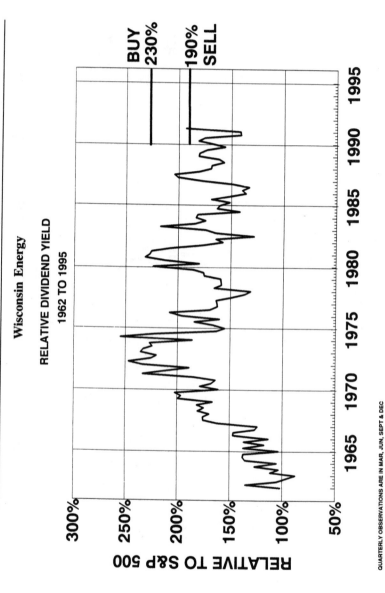

Wisconsin Energy

RELATIVE DIVIDEND YIELD

1962 TO 1995

QUARTERLY OBSERVATIONS ARE IN MAR, JUN, SEPT & DEC

FIGURE C-95

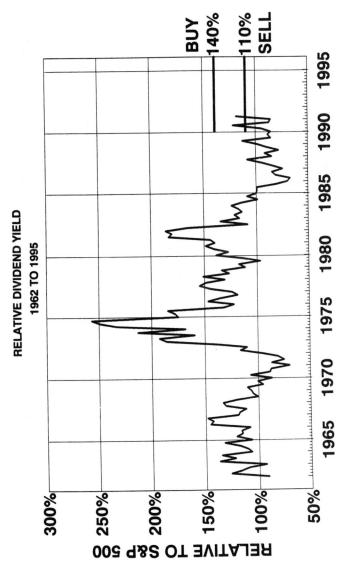

Woolworth

RELATIVE DIVIDEND YIELD
1962 TO 1995

QUARTERLY OBSERVATIONS ARE IN MAR, JUN, SEPT & DEC

269

Index

271